OPTING OUT: CHOICE AND THE FUTURE OF SCHOOLS

OPTING OUT

CHOICE AND THE FUTURE OF SCHOOLS

MARTIN ROGERS

LAWRENCE AND WISHART
LONDON

Lawrence & Wishart Ltd.
144a Old South Lambeth Road
London SW8 1XX

ISBN 0 85315 769 3

First published 1992

Cover design by Jan Brown Designs
Photoset by Art Services, Norwich
Printed and bound by
The Cromwell Press Limited,
Broughton Gifford, Melksham, Wiltshire

CONTENTS

ACKNOWLEDGEMENTS

This book could not have been written without my experience at Local Schools Information, a small and very busy organisation in which ideas are shared constantly.

I would therefore like to acknowledge the contribution made to the book by my colleagues Gaynor Kidd and (more recently) Pat Stevens, who have not only kept the unit smoothly administered but also joined in discussions.

Sandra Mohamed, my fellow information officer at LSI, has made a particular contribution. Sandra and I have travelled the length and breadth of England and Wales since 1989 speaking at around 300 meetings, and have developed our thinking jointly during the intervening spells in the office (whenever we could get off the phone!). The success of LSI has been the result of shared effort and enthusiasm.

I would also like to thank the many other colleagues, from a wide variety of backgrounds, who have provided information and encouragement both for work on the book and at LSI, and the staff of the Department for Education for their courtesy and efficiency in response to enquiries.

My thanks also to friends and family for putting up with the signs of stress and the lack of proper attention; finally to Tony and Frank, for help with the technology that made it possible.

GLOSSARY

Glossary of abbreviations and commonly occuring educational terms.

ASB Aggregated School Budget. The amount a LEA has left to distribute to the maintained schools (including those which have opted out) in its area through its LMS formula after deducting the value of 'excepted items'.

AWPU Age Weighted Pupil Unit. The 'cash value' of each pupil in a particular financial year. This is the basis of calculation of each school's formula-funded 'budget share' under LMS.

Budget Share. The amount a school receives through the formula, for which the governing body has delegated responsibility under LMS.

Capital. Expenditure of a non-recurrent kind (eg. building works or major equipment purchases).

Capitation. Money spent on books, materials and equipment (usually expressed, or calculated, per pupil).

CEO Chief Education Officer. A LEA is obliged to appoint a CEO; many LEAs now call this position 'Director of Education'.

County School. A school built, maintained and staffed by a LEA, the full cost being met from public funds.

Note: definitions include the use of terms that have their own entry in the glossary; organisations are listed separately in an appendix.

Curriculum. The programme of work and activities which a school provides for its pupils (of which the National Curriculum must form part in LEA and GM schools).

DES   Department of Education & Science. The name (until 6 July 1992) of the government ministry responsible for education in England and Wales. (DES is used in this book only when giving a reference of which the term is a part; otherwise, Department for Education or DFE is used throughout.)

DFE   Department For Education. The new name (from 6 July 1992) for the education ministry for England and Wales

Educational Psychologists. Professionals with both teaching and psychology degrees. Their work is generally directed towards enabling children to receive educational opportunities appropriate to their individual needs; they also arrange the formal assessment of the special educational needs of selected children.

Educational Welfare Officer/Service. Provides a link between school and home to help children (especially those from families facing particular problems) gain as much benefit as possible from the educational opportunities available to them. School attendance is a major - and statutory - part of this work.

ERA Education Reform Act 1988

'Excepted Items'. Items of LEA expenditure which are excepted from delegation in LMS schemes and are provided to schools directly by the LEA.

GM Grant-maintained

GSB General Schools Budget. The amount a LEA has to spend on maintained (including GM) schools in its area, including the costs of centrally-provided services ('excepted items').

HMI Her Majesty's Inspectorate/Inspector. The national inspectorate body which carries out various statutory duties on behalf of the Secretary of State and advises the Government on the education service.

LEA Local Education Authority. An elected local council which has responsibility for administering the education service within its area.

LMS Local Management of Schools. (Explained in detail in Chapter 2.)

Maintained School. A school for which the day-to-day running costs are paid by a LEA (includes 'county' and 'voluntary' schools).

NOC No Overall Control. Describing a LEA where no party has an overall majority; also known as a 'hung' council.

PSB Potential Schools Budget. A LEA's 'General Schools Budget' less certain items which may not be delegated to school level; basically, a guide to the amount a LEA could delegate under LMS.

Special School. A school for pupils with severe, complex or long-term special educational needs.

SSA Standard Spending Assessment. The sum of money that the Government believes a council needs to spend to provide a standard level of service.

TES Times Educational Supplement. A weekly specialist publication.

Voluntary School. A school built by a 'voluntary body' (usually a church or charitable trust) but maintained by a LEA. There are three types of voluntary school: aided; controlled and special agreement. Voluntary Aided are by far the most numerous, and include most of the church schools. The governors are responsible for providing, and maintaining the fabric of, the premises (but may get grants from the DFE). They also employ most of the staff, but the LEA pays for them - along with the other day-to-day costs.

INTRODUCTION

Education is the most widely used, and costly, of our public services. School provision is the largest part of the service, educating about seven million pupils; employing about 400,000 teachers, and a great many other staff; and costing around £14.5 billion in 1991-92. Around ninety-three per cent of children are educated in the state sector.

The present system of provision, and its form of organisation, are the result of a number of pieces of legislation going back to the last century, which are considered in the second chapter. However, the last decade has seen an unprecedented amount of schools legislation, the most radical changes arising from the Education Reform Act 1988. This introduced the National Curriculum and changes to religious education; Local Management of Schools (LMS), which requires a great deal of financial and management responsibility to be delegated to governing bodies; Open Enrolment, which reduces the power of local education authorities to plan admission levels for schools; Grant-Maintained Schools (i.e. opting out) and City Technology Colleges (CTCs).

There have been six Secretaries of State for Education and sixteen pieces of education legislation enacted since the Conservatives came to power in 1979. The White Paper published in July 1992 (preceding yet another Bill) was described by the new Education Secretary, John Patten, as:

> the last piece of the jigsaw to bring the new organisational framework together, taking account of the grant-maintained revolution. It will provide a clear statement of how we expect education to be over the next twenty-five years[1].

This book is primarily concerned with opting out and 'choice' but, as we shall see, open enrolment and LMS are essential aspects of the context. Some of the changes introduced by the 1988 Act - especially opting out - were seen as highly contentious at the time, and were opposed by most of those involved with schools.

By the time of the 1992 general election there were still only 219 grant-maintained (GM) schools. That number will now increase and, since the election, there has been widespread - but often ill-informed - speculation about the extent of that increase. Opting out is a choice open to most schools, and is an issue that a great many will undoubtedly consider over the next year or two. The results from the schools which have debated the issue since the election make it clear that they will not all reach the same conclusion; there are very mixed - and sometimes very strong - feelings on the subject.

If there were a widespread extension of opting out, of the order intended by the Government, it would bring about major changes to the school service that would affect all schools, and all those who learn or work in them now and in the future. Yet such changes have never been widely considered or publicly debated. As more schools consider opting out, following publication of the White Paper and a new Schools Bill, it is not only inevitable that the consequences will be debated, but essential that they are understood on the broadest level achievable. It is now possible to draw on the current experience of opting out and the Local Management of Schools when discussing the likely effect of these changes - which was not, of course, a possibility during the very limited 'consultation' that preceded the introduction of these measures.

This book is written not only for parents, governors, and those professionally involved, but for anyone with an interest in the school system and its future. The community as a whole provides and pays for state schools; the well-being, both social and economic, of the nation depends in large part on the success of the school system.

That ought to keep the book at the top of the best-seller list for months; but of course it won't, for only a small proportion of those affected by the education service (as with medicine, law and other professions) take an active interest in its operation. Most of us are far too ready to leave such activity and responsibility to others, whilst (of course) reserving our right to complain and criticise. We are too inclined to accept the views of 'experts' without examining their evidence - if any - and too prone to subjecting complex systems to simple 'solutions', and expecting swift results.

Politicians, subject as they are to roughly four-year election cycles, are particularly guilty of raising such expectations, yet education is self-evidently a long-term process: each child is obliged by law to receive at least eleven years of it. Whatever remedies are applied to whatever problems (whether real or imagined - or politically expedient), it must be obvious to any thoughtful observer that it will take years to judge the effects; and that any effect can only be judged accurately by an intelligent assessment of valid evidence.

It is a strange paradox that, when children start attending school they are encouraged to observe, measure and compare and then to draw conclusions by thoughtful analysis of the evidence they have collected; adults, however, when they start attending to schools, frequently rely on hypothesis, prejudice and dogma - often in the face of such evidence as does exist.

In looking at the school system, and particularly the way in which opting out could radically alter it, I have, therefore, sought and referred to evidence wherever possible. I shall raise the sort of basic questions that a child might ask, which are too often dismissed by adults either because we have no ready answers, or because they challenge the very view we are putting forward. All of us must have experienced the difficulty, and sometimes discomfort, of answering the question 'Why?' from a small child.

Having worked since 1989 at Local Schools Information, a unit established specifically to advise on and monitor opting out, I naturally have my own views - which will surely show. However, throughout the unit's existence, during which period my colleague, Sandra Mohamed, and I have attended some three hundred meetings in schools considering the issue, we have sought to present accurate, factual information in a rational and comprehensible form. We have made contact with hundreds of headteachers, thousands of governors and tens of thousands of parents. We have heard a huge range of views expressed and, in offering our own, have frequently contributed to a healthy debate before decisions have been made. That is as it should be.

The purpose of this book is the same: to stimulate and help inform the much-needed and long-overdue public debate on the way our schools are managed and governed, as well as to assist those with a specific interest in the issue of opting out. I do not want it to be read only by people who share my views. Indeed, I hope it will be read with an open mind by a great variety of individuals, and that it will contribute in some way to the (re)establishment of a broad consensus about the future of our school service.

The White Paper was published on 28 July 1992, after the main text of the book was written. It is therefore discussed separately, in Chapter 10, although amendments have been made elsewhere to take account of its contents.

As I have said, the book is aimed at a wide variety of readers, some of whom will come to it better informed than others. My intention is that anyone with an interest in the subject should find the book useful and that I will not lose readers on the way by assuming knowledge they do not possess. A particular source of difficulty is the extent to which those already involved in the service are familiar with, and use, its jargon - especially acronyms and initials. A glossary of commonly-used terms and abbreviations is included for reference and, throughout the text, new terms are introduced with an explanation. It is probably possible to write a document on the education service which hardly includes a recognisable word of 'ordinary English'. I have tried to avoid this as far as possible.

I am aware of the extent to which this book could have covered more fully some of the issues which are secondary to its main theme; time is a ruthless constraint! The author would welcome comments from readers, which would doubtless be valuable for any revised edition that may appear.

NOTE

1 *Guardian*, 19.5.92.

1
WHAT IS OPTING OUT?

This chapter sketches the basic outlines of opting out and points to the issues that arise through the process. A more detailed analysis of the procedures, and the associated issues, follows in subsequent chapters.

The 1988 Education Reform Act provided for the creation of a new type of school: the Grant-Maintained School. A grant-maintained school can only be created from an existing school maintained by a Local Education Authority (LEA). The Secretary of State for Education must approve the school's application for grant-maintained status, as a result of which it is removed from the LEA to be run entirely by its (new) governing body and headteacher. It is then funded by grants paid by the Department for Education (DFE).[1] The main grant is the Annual Maintenance Grant, the value of which is recovered from the LEA. Secondary, middle and primary schools may apply to opt out; nursery and special schools are not eligible at present, though the White Paper proposes to enable special schools to opt out in due course.

A ballot of the parents of children registered as pupils of the school decides whether or not to apply for GM status; in other words, whether to remain within the established LEA system or to 'opt out' of it.

The ballot may be initiated either by a resolution of the governing body (by far the most common way so far) or by a petition of parents submitted to the governing body. It is a postal ballot, conducted by the Electoral Reform Society. Provided that more than half of the eligible parents take part, the result is decisive; if fewer than half take part, a second ballot must be held at once - the result of which is decisive regardless of the 'turnout'. If the majority of those voting is opposed to opting out, that is the end of the matter for a period of, normally, at least a year. If the majority is in favour, the governing body is then under a duty to prepare, publish and submit to the Secretary of State its application for GM status within six months of the ballot. There is then a two month period during which objections to the proposals may be submitted, after which the Secretary of State may make his (or her)[2] decision.

A key part of the application is the proposed initial governing body for the school should it become grant-maintained, which may or may not include many of the present governors. The Act prescribes the composition of the governing body of a GM school as follows:

the headteacher

one or two elected teacher governors

five elected parent governors

a number of others* which *must* outnumber the others by at least one and are appointed. This group must include representation of the business community and at least two people who are parents of registered pupils *at the time of their appointment.*

If the application is approved, the initial governing body will be given certain 'transitional powers' relating to the school once it has acquired GM status; other functions during the transitional period (which may be weeks or months) remain with the original governing body.

The funding of GM schools is by grant from the Department for Education. The day-to-day running costs are

---

* The members of this, appointed, group are termed 'first' governors if the school is a 'county' (ie. 'normal' LEA) school and 'foundation' governors if the school is a 'voluntary' (church or charitable trust) school (further details are given in Chapter 4).

paid by an Annual Maintenance Grant, which consists of: the 'formula funding' that the school would have received under the Local Management of Schools scheme were it still within the LEA; an element to compensate the school for the loss of centrally-provided LEA services (to which it is no longer entitled as a GM school - but may purchase); and an element towards the cost of providing midday meals. In addition, there are other grants for which the school may apply: capital grants for building work and 'special purpose grants' for a number of other purposes - mostly those for which the Department for Education funds LEAs. The value of the annual maintenance grant of each GM school is recovered by the government from the LEA it opted out of; the cost of other grants to GM schools is covered by a reduction in the level of funding to LEAs generally.

The levels of these grants, including the additional element of the annual maintenance grant for centrally-provided services, are set annually. The figures for the following financial year are normally announced by the government around October; so when opting out is being considered in a school, it is generally impossible to predict what a school would actually receive if it did opt out. The closest one can get - and in the next year or so especially, that may turn out to be not very close at all - is to say what it would have got if it had been a GM school during the financial year in which the decision is being taken. For this reason, even strong advocates of opting out warn that the prospect of a 'pot of gold' is neither sufficient, nor the right, reason for doing it. Yet, it is undoubtedly the lure of the extra funding that has been paid to schools opting out in the early stages of the policy that has continued to attract further schools; it is certainly the factor that is most frequently, and most prominently, presented to parents to encourage them to support opting out. We shall return to the issue of funding in more detail later.

What are the other major changes that occur as a result

of a school opting out? The governing body becomes the owner of the school site and buildings and, thereby, responsible for them - and for the safety of those who use and work in them. (The debt charges arising from the creation of the school, however, remain with the LEA to be borne by local tax payers.) The governing body becomes the employer of the staff and thus responsible for all aspects of employment practice. (Staff have no choice over the transfer of their employment contracts from the LEA to the governing body, other than to resign and seek a job elsewhere if they are not happy with the change. Staff in voluntary-aided schools are already employed by the governing body, so it is not such a change for them.) The governing body also becomes responsible for the admissions policy of the school and its implementation - including appeals against non-admission. It becomes responsible, also, for appeals against the exclusion of pupils (ie. suspensions and expulsions).

The LEA retains responsibility for the provision of a number of services to individual pupils in GM schools (as opposed to services to the whole school) on the same basis as they are provided to pupils in LEA-maintained schools These are:

the assessment of, and provision for, the special educational needs of children (under the 1981 Education Act)

education psychology and education welfare services

health and dental services

the provision of clothing/uniform grants

home-to-school transport

a careers service

All the changes outlined above mark the transfer of

responsibility from the LEA to the governing body. In the event of some problem arising over any of them, the next stop becomes either the courts or the Secretary of State, rather than the local education office or local councillor. Whilst the changes introduced by the 1988 Act were generally claimed to be devolutionary in nature, they actually move responsibility away from LEAs in two directions: downwards to the level of the school, and upwards to the level of the central government. All these matters are considered in more detail in later chapters; their significance should already be clear.

In order to understand the nature of the changes introduced by GM status, it is first necessary to understand the way in which a school is now run within an LEA, and the system from which it may opt out. The following chapter covers the origins and evolution of the present system and gives an account of the Local Management of Schools (LMS) and Open Enrolment - both of which, like GM status, were introduced in the 1988 Act. Although LMS is, therefore, only in the relatively early stages of refinement, the rate of change has been remarkable - and is likely to take a further leap forward in the next year.

NOTES

1 The ministry responsible for education changed its name on 6 July 1992 from the Department of Education and Science (DES) to the Department for Education (DFE).

2 Legislation, which is drafted and passed predominantly by men, always refers to the Secretary of State as a male. Solely in the interests of simplicity, the same convention is followed hereafter.

2

THE PRESENT SCHOOL SYSTEM

In England and Wales responsibility for the education service
is distributed between central government, local education
authorities (LEAs), the churches and other voluntary bodies, the
governing bodies of educational institutions, and the teaching
profession. The service can be described, therefore, as a national
system locally administered.[1]

That description, from the government's own Education
Department, still applies at the moment. A key issue arising
from current changes is whether it should continue to apply
and, if not, what should replace it? Could the replacement
still be described as a system, and what would be the effect
on the level and quality of service available to the majority
of children?

Arriving at the present position has taken almost a
century, and several Education Acts between 1870 and
1944. It is easy to forget how relatively recent is the school
system we now take largely for granted.

Before 1870, most 'elementary schools' - which were
the only form of widely available schooling, and catered for
children from the age of five - had been provided by the
churches. The 1870 (Forster) Elementary Education Act
established universal provision for the first time, and created
local School Boards responsible for elementary education in
their areas, including the building of new schools (many of
which are still in use). These were financed from both local
rates and national taxes. By the start of this century, most
children attended such schools until the age of twelve.
(Many of the 'all-age' elementary schools were organised
with separate infant and senior departments, the latter often
segregating girls and boys; the surviving buildings often
display the architectural evidence of the original entrances.)

The government body overseeing developments was the Committee of the Privy Council on Education, until its replacement in 1899 by a national Board of Education for England and Wales.

The 1902 (Balfour) Act replaced the School Boards, passing responsibility to County and County Borough Councils as local education authorities. A number of these subsequently used their powers (and they were powers, not duties) to establish secondary schools on the rates. Whilst these schools charged fees, they also offered scholarships to pupils from elementary schools. The 1902 Act also introduced, controversially, financial assistance to church schools from the rates.

The 1918 (Fisher) Act strengthened the role of central government and raised the school leaving age to fourteen, though not until 1922. In the years between the wars, there was pressure - but little money - for further reform. The 'Hadow' Report[2] of 1926 proposed the reorganisation of all elementary schools into three stages: infant (five to seven), junior (seven to eleven) and senior (eleven to fourteen). It also recommended the raising of the leaving age to fifteen and that *all* children should go into some form of secondary education (rather than the ten per cent or so that did at the time). In addition the report suggested the division of post-eleven education into grammar schools and 'modern' schools, with 'senior classes' in elementary schools for pupils unable to attend a secondary school (often because there were none sufficiently local).

By the outbreak of war in 1939 about half of elementary school pupils were still in the old all-age schools. Almost two-thirds of pupils over eleven were in reorganised schools, mainly in urban areas, but still only about fifteen per cent of eleven-year-olds went from elementary to secondary schools. There was a difference in school regulations covering secondary and elementary schools, with inferior standards (and lower salaries for teachers) in the latter; so the large majority of pupils over eleven were still not receiving a good secondary education. In addition, the recommendation to raise the leaving age had not been implemented.

The Spens Report[3] of 1938 recommended that all post-primary education should be brought under secondary school regulations; that there should be three types of secondary school - grammar, technical and modern (it rejected, 'reluctantly', the idea of providing all three types of education by streaming within single 'multilateral' schools); that the leaving age should be raised to sixteen as soon as possible; and that fees should be abolished. These recommendations were not implemented at the time, but the foundations for the 1944 Act were clearly becoming visible as war broke out.

The demands of war, not only for considerably increased industrial output, but for rapid technological development, starkly demonstrated the inadequacies of this level of education; the response to these demands, however, demonstrated the extent to which huge numbers of people had capabilities that had previously found little opportunity for expression. The pressure for a much better, and more equitable, system of education provision was irresistable. The experience of war, the resourcefulness it stimulated - not least in schools which, deprived of resources, were developing new approaches to a pupil population greatly disrupted through evacuation, from a teaching force greatly disrupted by military service - and the much greater mixing of social classes made substantial change inevitable. The Board of Education established a committee to work on post-war education reconstruction to meet this demand. A White Paper, *Educational Reconstruction*, was published in July 1943, followed by an Education Bill in December. These were the product of some two and a half years of patient consultation and negotiation by R.A.Butler and his Parliamentary Secretary

Chuter Ede, particularly over arrangements acceptable to the churches over their position in a 'dual system' of church and state school provision. The Act received the Royal Assent on 4 August 1944.

Butler's 1944 Education Act is generally accepted as a major achievement of consensus. It was, of course, the product of a coalition wartime government and certainly included sufficient compromise for most interested parties to find in it much of what they sought. It has stood the test of time sufficiently well for its reforms to be largely intact, albeit modified, almost fifty years later.

The major development was the introduction of secondary education for all which, since now compulsory, was also to be provided free of charge. The Board of Education became a Ministry, the new Minister having a duty 'to promote the education of the people of England and Wales and the progressive development of institutions devoted to that purpose'. (Responsibility for Wales was transferred to the Secretary of State for Wales in subsequent legislation.)

The system was organised into primary, secondary and further education sectors and LEAs were put under a duty to ensure that sufficient provision existed to meet the needs of the population of their area. The school leaving age was raised to fifteen (implemented in 1947), with the long-term objective (not realised until 1972) of raising it to sixteen. The Act retained the dual system of church and LEA provision by 'trading' an increased level of public funding for church schools for an increased level of local democratic influence on them through the governing bodies. Voluntary schools now became 'aided' or, in fewer cases, 'controlled' schools.

Whilst 'multilateral' (non-selective) secondary schools - the fore-runners of comprehensives, for which there had been growing support - became a possibility for the first time, the pattern clearly envisaged was the tripartite system of grammar, technical and modern schools. The Act also made it the duty of parents to ensure that their children received full-time education suitable to their 'age, ability and aptitude'. It required ministerial and LEA powers and duties to be exercised 'so far as is compatible with the provision of efficient instruction and training and the avoidance of unreasonable public expenditure', and having regard to the general principle that pupils should be educated in accordance with the wishes of their parents.

In fact, the system that evolved was largely bipartite, as few technical schools were established. Grammar schools were inevitably seen to have a higher status than the secondary moderns. A growing disenchantment with selection at eleven led to a number of LEAs reorganising along comprehensive lines in the early 1960s. Edward Boyle, the (Conservative) Minister of Education announced in 1963 that the time had come to abandon the bipartite system as the norm. In the same year, the Labour Party adopted as policy comprehensive reorganisation and the abolition of the eleven-plus examination. In July 1965 Circular 10/65 was issued by the then (Labour) Secretary of State for Education, Anthony Crosland, requesting LEAs to submit their reorganisation proposals for comprehensive education within a year. Thus, the introduction of comprehensive education in the secondary sector was initiated at local level in response to public demand, and then urged upon LEAs more generally. However, the fact that this was done in the form of a 'request' meant that whilst many authorities, across the political spectrum, introduced comprehensive schooling eagerly, others did not do so at all.

The withdrawal of Circular 10/65 shortly became a manifesto commitment of the Conservatives, and was duly executed by the new Education Secretary, Margaret Thatcher, following their victory in June 1970. However, despite this early symbolic signal, Mrs Thatcher actually presided over the closure of more grammar schools as a result of comprehensive reorganisation than any other Secretary of State before or since. Whilst it has always been easy to find supporters of grammar schools, it has never been possible to find the (politically) necessary equal (let alone greater) numbers of supporters for the re-introduction of secondary moderns. Indeed, on each of the few occasions that an authority has sought to re-open this debate by proposing to open a new grammar school, the opposition has been overwhelming. However, as Secretary of State, Mrs Thatcher could, and did, obstruct the closure of a number of grammar schools - and thus blocked the introduction of truly comprehensive systems in several areas. In the intervening years, only a small minority of LEAs have retained partially selective systems; there are around one hundred and fifty grammar schools left in England and Wales. However, at the very time of writing, the issue has been raised again by a proposal to consult on the opening of a grammar school in Milton Keynes - the only area of Buckinghamshire to provide a completely comprehensive secondary school system. The Education Committee approved the proposal by a single vote, but it was rejected by a clear majority by the full county council.

Within the context of this book, we have concentrated in this section on the way legislation affected the organisation of provision. There was also much debate, particularly during and since the 1960s, about the curriculum in both primary and secondary sectors. The main issue in the former was the development of 'child-centred' (as opposed to the traditional, largely 'rote') learning. In the secondary sector there was growing concern over the extent to which the curriculum was dominated by - or modelled upon - the requirements of the tiny minority of secondary pupils who were destined to progress to university; these were increasingly recognised as having little relevance to the majority of pupils. However, as the National Curriculum (introduced in the 1988 Act) applies to all state schools - including those which opt out of their LEA - it is not strictly relevant to our area of concern.

Other Education Acts and reports that have altered, or sought to influence, the system of governance of schools, or have particular relevance to the acknowledged position of parents within the education system, are considered in Chapter 4.

The next major reform of the school system was Kenneth Baker's Education Reform Act of 1988, the main ingredients of which were the National Curriculum and the testing at fixed stages of Standard Attainment Targets (SATs); changes to religious education and the requirements for collective worship in schools; Local Management of Schools and Open Enrolment (discussed below); Grant-Maintained Schools (opting out); and City Technology Colleges.

City Technology Colleges (CTCs) are another new type of school. The Government's intention was that they should actually be created as new schools (rather than from the modification of existing schools), and that they would be sponsored by capital funds from industry - which, in return, would benefit from the partnership thus established and, particularly, from the emphasis on technology within their curriculum. Like private independent schools, they are not bound by the National Curriculum. However, as state schools (with their running costs met by government grant), they provide free education to their pupils, who are selected on the basis of aptitude. They were to be located, as their name implies, in inner city areas, to provide opportunities for local children and to challenge the monopoly of provision of the local authorities. The original plan envisaged twenty such institutions, but a marked reluctance on the part of industry - notably the large, prestigious companies - to come forward with the necessary sponsorship or, indeed, to have anything to do with the scheme, has left it well short of the original target. There are now just fifteen City Technology Colleges open or definitely due to open; several are founded on existing schools; some are not in inner city areas and many have required a far greater injection of public funds than was intended. The Government, however, has persisted with its enthusiasm for the idea, and the new White Paper proposes various derivatives, which are described in Chapter 10.

The origins and background of opting out, and the opening of the system to market forces as a matter of policy, is the subject of the next chapter. For now, we shall look at how schools are presently run, and financed, as a result of the changes introduced by the 1988 Act.

LOCAL MANAGEMENT OF SCHOOLS (LMS)

LMS has completely altered the system of funding and managing schools. By the introduction of a formula for calculating school budgets and requirements for the delegation of financial and management responsibility to governing bodies, it has shifted a great deal of decision-making to school level. It was based on work that had been done in a number of LEAs - notably Cambridgeshire - and was originally known as Local Financial Management. It is worth looking in some detail at LMS as it is the system under which LEA schools now operate and, therefore, the one with which GM status needs to be compared.

The official circular on LMS (DES 7/88) described it as follows:

> Local management of schools represents a major challenge and a major opportunity for the education service. The introduction of needs-based formula funding and the delegation of financial and managerial responsibilities to governing bodies are key elements in the Government's overall policy to improve the quality of teaching and learning in schools. Local management is concerned with far more than budgeting and accounting

procedures. Effective schemes of local management will enable governing bodies and head teachers to plan their use of resources - including their most valuable resource, their staff - to maximum effect in accordance with their own needs and priorities, and to make schools more responsive to their clients - parents, pupils, the local community and employers.

The underlying principle of schemes of local management is to secure the maximum delegation of financial and managerial responsibilities to governing bodies that is consistent with the discharge by the Secretary of State and by the LEA of their continuing statutory responsibilities. A limited number of services will continue to be provided centrally by the LEA, but only where that is clearly demonstrated to be more efficient or effective. Each LEA's scheme - and in particular the basis for allocating resources between individual schools - should be as simple and clear as possible, so that governors, staff and the local community are fully aware of how it operates.

It must be remembered that LMS itself is still being developed and refined, and that some of the early schools to opt out did so even before its introduction - so many of the advantages they have claimed for opting out are, in fact, advantages of LMS, upon which GM status is based. The evolution of LMS has been by a series of steps taken at the start of each financial year since its introduction - nobody gets thanked for making changes mid-year. As this process is not yet complete, no school in any LEA is yet in a position to make a comparison between GM status and LMS in its final form.

The degree of change brought about by LMS is described below. The rate of change has, necessarily, been extremely fast, and schemes will be modified further, into a more or less final form, over the next couple of years. Schools which opt out of LEAs lose their right to be included in the process of consultation over further changes in LMS, but will continue to be affected by them, since their budgets are, at present, primarily dependent on the the LMS funding formula. LEAs, meanwhile, will be under no obligation to take account of particular difficulties that GM schools may face as a result of the formula. The effect of any further changes, which will be in the direction of further devolution, will be to reduce the differences between GM and LMS schools. Some LEAs are already proposing levels of delegation and arrangements over service provision that will virtually eliminate the differences altogether.

Prior to LMS, the level of resourcing of schools had been determined by the decisions of LEA education committees according to a variety of criteria - often complex and subject to local factors (including lobbying and political considerations) and, as a result, not always readily open to public scrutiny and interpretation. These LEA decisions generally included detailed allocations of staffing (both teaching and non-teaching), capitation (ie. the money for books, equipment, etc.) and additional services. Some LEAs included a sum over which the school had discretion but, otherwise, schools had little or no control, or even influence, over the way in which their budgets were spent. They may not even have known the actual value of their budget. The LEA itself may well have had no accurate idea of the value of individual school budgets, as its own expenditure would have been managed under budget heads that were 'service-led' rather than 'institution-led' (in other words, built up from the costs of different aspects of service provision, rather than the costs of individual institutions).

This situation was completely transformed by the requirements of LMS, under which the budget of each school is determined according to a formula that applies across the whole LEA. Budgets - along with a number of associated management responsibilities - are delegated to school governing bodies. LEAs were obliged to draw up a 'scheme' for LMS, according to criteria laid down by the Government, and submit them to the Secretary of State for approval. Resistance to some of these criteria led to a number of schemes being turned down until modified; we shall return shortly to the details of the requirements - which many still consider to have serious flaws.

Before looking more closely at LMS and how it operates, it is worth looking back at a couple of the sentences from the circular to highlight the context into which opting out should be put:

> The underlying principle of schemes of local management is to secure *the maximum delegation of financial and managerial responsibilities to governing bodies that is consistent with the discharge by the Secretary of State and by the LEA of their continuing statutory responsibilities*. A limited number of services will continue to be provided centrally by the LEA, *but only where that is clearly demonstrated to be more efficient or effective*.

Two questions arise from this: firstly, what significant additional responsibilities (and therefore powers or independence) can be gained by opting out as opposed to LMS once fully implemented? Secondly, if the only LEA-provided services are to be those '*clearly demonstrated to be more efficient or effective*' if provided by the authority, what advantage can exist in opting out, which could reduce the school's access to such services (or, at least, would oblige the school to pay for them at commercial rates)?

If opting out is the most radical measure in the 1988 Act, LMS is certainly the most wide-reaching. It brought about a fundamental shift in the distribution of powers and responsibilities for the management of the education service, away from the LEA to individual school level, in line with the philosophy of placing decision-making as close as possible to those affected by the decisions. The role of the LEA has been much reduced, and is still changing as a result of more recent legislation. It is now less concerned with the day-to-day affairs of schools and is concentrated instead on a number of strategic areas: the determination of overall budget provision (subject to the increasing control of central government); monitoring schools' delivery of education, and their effectiveness; planning the pattern of provision (of which, more later); informing the community about local provision; and protecting the rights of individuals.

Coupled with Open Enrolment (see below), LMS effectively introduces a 'voucher' system into the state school service, which is consistent with this government's philosophy of provision being determined wherever possible by the operation of market forces. This development, and the part that opting out plays in it, is discussed later.

The introduction of LMS took place in a very short time, and still quite recently. It is hardly surprising, considering the scale of change involved, that the process is not yet complete. Indeed, it was always the intention that it would take a period of years to complete the transition.

The 1988 Act was passed in July of that year; LEAs were given only until September 1989 to prepare their schemes for LMS, consult the governing bodies and headteachers of every school affected and submit their draft schemes to the Secretary of State for approval. (The new LEAs established as a result of the abolition of the Inner London Education Authority - also by the 1988 Act - were given two years longer.) A scheme consists of two separate, but related, aspects: formula funding and the delegation of budgets and responsibilities. We shall now look at these in more detail.

LMS SCHEMES

LEAs' overall school budgets had to be disaggregated (broken down) to the level of individual primary and secondary schools (nursery and special schools were initially excluded from LMS, though special schools are now being brought in). Each school's running costs had, in future, to be determined according to a formula for the allocation of the total resources available.

Starting with the LEA's whole budget for schools, the

General Schools Budget, a number of 'excepted items' - those which continue to be provided by the authority - were deducted. The remainder is called the Aggregated Schools Budget. Some of the exceptions are 'mandatory' (ie. compulsory), for example capital expenditure and home-to-school transport; others are 'discretionary' (ie. the LEA can choose whether or not to make the item an exception). Discretionary items were further sub-divided into those without a limit, for example school meals, and others which were limited initially to ten per cent of the Aggregated Schools Budget, reducing to seven per cent, for example structural maintenance and library and museum services.

Having deducted the exceptions, the remaining 'Aggregated Schools Budget' is distributed to schools according to the LEA's formula. The formula is age-weighted (because it is more expensive to educate some age-groups than others) and needs-related (because schools vary in their circumstances: small schools require enhanced staffing; premises costs vary greatly; some have more pupils requiring additional support than others). Overall, at least seventy-five per cent of the ASB had to be distributed according to pupil numbers, taking account of the age-weighting factor, with no more than twenty-five per cent being based on different levels of need. Each school's LMS budget (known as its 'Budget Share' or 'formula funding') is then calculated by multiplying the 'Age-Weighted Pupil Unit (AWPU) for each age group by the number of pupils in that age group on the roll of the school. The new system has been graphically described as each child bringing its own little bag of money to the school - and the replacement of children by AWPUs has been the subject of some regret by many concerned with schools.

Schools' new budgets under LMS may be, and often are, very different from historic levels of spending. Most schools, to a greater or lesser extent, are 'winners' or 'losers' in this process. In recognition of this, schemes are subject to transitional arrangements over the first four years to dampen the most dramatic effects of the change. Even so, major problems exist which, together with the effects of simultaneous cuts in LEA budgets (often under pressure from central government), have led to LMS being dubbed by some 'Less Money for Schools'. A consideration of these problems will be found later in this chapter.

In 1991, the regulations were changed and a new concept, the Potential Schools Budget (PSB) was introduced. The PSB is the General Schools Budget minus only the following exceptions: capital expenditure and debt charges; expenditure supported by central government and European Community grant; home to school transport; school meals and transitional excepted items. A new target was set, replacing the original arrangements for discretionary exceptions with a requirement to delegate eighty- five per cent of the PSB to schools by April 1994. Most LEAs were already ahead of this target, or close to it, by 1992. Also, the proportion that has to be allocated according to pupil numbers was increased from seventy-five to eighty per cent (reducing the maximum needs-based element to twenty per cent).

Within three years of the introduction of LMS schemes, responsibility for the management of their budgets had to be delegated to all secondary schools and to primary schools with more than two hundred pupils (and could be delegated to smaller primary schools if desired). Again, most LEAs had completed this process ahead of the target date.

Governing bodies, with advice from their headteachers, and training and support from LEAs, are now responsible for the overall management of their schools - including its budget - taking account of the general conditions and requirements of LEAs' schemes. The other major new role is the appointment and disciplining ('hiring and firing') of staff, in which governors had previously been involved, but without sole responsibility. The staffing complements, including grades and posts of responsibility, are now matters for the governing body to determine, within the constraints of their budget.

In the event of a major problem, an LEA may take back these powers - which are delegated, not absolute; as far as the author is aware, this has happened only once so far: a move by the governing body of Bridport County Primary School to initiate procedures to opt out of Dorset County Council provoked a petition from parents calling for the resignation of the governors (and the headteacher); the governors (and head) did resign - leaving the Council with little choice but to take back responsibility until the situation was resolved. The school did not opt out.

OPEN ENROLMENT

We shall deal more briefly with this issue, which is simpler and of less significance to opting out, as it applies equally to GM schools. Prior to the 1988 Act, LEAs were able to set the intake size of schools as part of their planning function. This was particularly significant during the late 1970s and 1980s, when a dramatic decline in pupil numbers followed the earlier drop in the birth rate. A substantial amount of surplus capacity arose in the school system as re-organisation (closure and/or amalgamation of schools) failed to keep pace with the decline in the pupil population. Given the time it takes to go through the procedures for re-organisation, the disruption it causes and the inevitability of the opposition that has to be overcome, this is hardly surprising. (Where there are objections, the approval of the Secretary of State is required. This has often been a cause of delay, and sometimes proposals are rejected. Obviously such plans are timed where possible to coincide with the school year, so even a short delay in decisions - at a critical time - can result in a year's delay in implementation.)

Whilst some of the surplus space was used to improve

35

the range of facilities in schools, and some was used for the development of other educational provision (those being happier economic times), much remained - and it was unevenly distributed between schools. The application of admission limits, which often bore little relation to physical capacity, meant that pupils were sometimes refused admission to schools even though they had spare accommodation. However, this was not a bureaucratic device to frustrate the wishes of parents; it was a valuable mechanism for maintaining viability across a range of schools and preventing a polarisation between crowded, popular schools and half-empty, unpopular ones.

Popularity, incidentally, may not just depend on quality - either real or perceived, academic or otherwise; it is, anyway, quite common for a school's reputation, good or bad, to be several years out of date and no longer justified. Atmosphere, location and accessibility, for example, are also likely to be major considerations for parents.

Open enrolment has changed all that. Each school now has a 'Standard Number' up to which all pupils applying must be admitted (unless it is a church school or operates an approved form of selection, in which case other criteria may override the requirements of open enrolment). Unless some variation has been approved by the Secretary of State, the standard number is either the number of pupils admitted to the school in 1979 or in 1989 - whichever is the higher. The intention is that it should be close to the physical capacity of the school. If the school is over-subscribed (ie. has more applicants than places), the admissions policy of the LEA (or school, if it is voluntary-aided or has opted out) will be used to determine which pupils will be admitted. In all cases of non-admittance, parents have the right of appeal to an independent panel (or, in a GM school, to a panel of governors with an additional independent element), the decision of which is binding. The Government has claimed that open enrolment brings a major extension of parental choice. Indeed, so much has been said about parents being able 'to choose the school they want' that many (not unreasonably) now expect their child to be admitted to the chosen school. It then comes as a blow to find that often they are not, because the intake has been filled by those with a stronger claim under the admissions policy. In this situation, parents are left with a choice only between those schools that still have space after the initial allocation. Since the introduction of open enrolment, probably because of the expectations raised, the number of appeals against non-admission has rocketed. Whilst it may be a good sign that parents are increasingly inclined to exercise their rights to appeal, it will achieve little so long as 'popular' schools are full (and therefore cannot take additional pupils). There is a real problem over the extent to which parents' expectations have been raised beyond a level at which they can be satisfied.

In yet another change, intended to defuse this situation to some extent, the allocation of capital funds from 1993/94 will make it possible for some popular schools (defined as those which have been over-subscribed by more than ten per cent for at least the three previous years) to expand *even in areas where there is overall surplus capacity*. (As a colleague observed, it will thus become possible for small schools - which are often more popular with parents - to meet demand by becoming large schools!) This is a further development in the replacement of planning by the application of market forces as the determining mechanism for establishing provision. However, in view of the current economic situation in the country, and the pressure from the Treasury to reduce public spending, it seems likely that very little money will be available for such purposes.

There is one major problem in the school system that could be made much worse rather than better by the move from planning to market forces in determining provision and that is the problem of 'failing schools' (sometimes disparagingly referred to as 'sink schools'). Under the new system of LMS, where funds are tightly related to pupil numbers and LEAs no longer have the power to appoint or remove staff, there is very little that an authority can do to support a school that is facing real difficulties. If, for whatever reason, a school experiences a drop in the number of pupils enrolling, it will suffer a cut in its budget. This will present the governing body with the need to reduce spending, probably by reducing staff. A downward spiral of confidence and resources can set in very quickly - and there is no apparent mechanism under the present system for reversing this process. The Government has announced that it intends to intervene in situations where schools are judged to be failing their pupils (see Chapter 10). The key differences between GM and LEA schools on admissions are that the policy of a GM school is determined by its governing body (subject to the approval of the Secretary of State) and, as has been mentioned, appeals against non-admission are heard by a panel of its governors, with an independent element, rather than a panel which is entirely independent of the school. This gives GM schools which are over-subscribed a greater degree of control over admissions than is the case in a LEA school.

FINANCIAL PROBLEMS OF LMS

Probably the greatest reason for discontent over the implementation of LMS has been the fact that it was introduced against a background of diminishing resources. It has therefore seemed as though the new responsibility given to school governors has not been to decide how to spend money - but how to save it. The nasty decisions about where to make cuts have now been devolved, rather than the pleasant task of deciding what additional items a school most needs. One effect of this has been to make it much harder for anyone to see who is really responsible for any inadequacies that arise: central government, the local authority or even the governors themselves. A cynical observer might believe this is not accidental. Even the House of Commons Select Committee on Education said:

> Local authorities in England spend nearly three times as much on education as central government - almost £18 billion in 1990-91. In considering this huge block of expenditure we face two related problems: information and accountability ... *We urge the Government to clarify the present confusion of accountability, where central and local government can blame each other for spending deficiencies and other policy failures and where the scrutiny of expenditure is virtually impossible.*[4] (The emphasis is that of the Committee's report.)

Through recent changes to the whole system of local government finance - details of which are beyond the scope of this book, but a basic grasp of which is very useful - the Government now effectively controls what councils are able to spend. Councils' main income is from a mixture of central government grant, a share of the National Non-Domestic Rate and local tax paid by residents. (There have been three forms of local tax - that is tax raised by councils - in recent years: Rates, which were replaced by the Poll Tax/Community Charge which, in turn, has been replaced by the Council Tax. For simplicity, I use the term 'local tax' to cover all three.) The Government decides, through a complex procedure, in which many councils (and others) have little confidence, what it believes each council needs to spend in order to provide a standard level of service. These are the 'Standard Spending Assessments' (SSAs). There is a Standard Spending Assessment for each major service, and a catch-all for 'other services'. By totalling these, the Government (through the Department of the Environment) arrives at an overall SSA for each council - in other words, what the Government believes its budget should be. It deducts from the SSA what the council will receive from the National Non-Domestic Rate (NNDR - the unified business rate which replaced the local business rates) and what it would raise from local tax at the level the Government wishes it to be set. The balance is funded centrally by Revenue Support Grant.

The Government cannot control what a council actually spends on any particular service; that is, how it divides its overall budget between the various areas of provision it makes. It cannot even control what services a council actually provides (each LEA, for example, receives a component of its education SSA for nursery education, but some provide hardly any). These are matters for councils to decide for themselves, but the fact that SSAs are published creates its own pressure, as the information will be used by all sorts of interested parties to apply pressure on the councils, especially where they are spending at a level below their Standard Spending Assessment on a particular service. The problem is that not only is the whole basis of SSAs questionable, but the system now runs against the principle of local democracy that was claimed to underly the local tax. When first introduced, it was argued that the Poll Tax would give councils - and their electorates - a choice between high spending with high local taxation or low spending with low local taxation. The level of spending would reflect both the level of services provided and the efficiency of those services, and the different political parties would be able to put their own proposals before the electorate.

Any difference between the Government's assessment of what a council should spend and the council's own higher assessment of what it wishes, or needs, to spend can only be funded through the local tax (now that business rates are centrally distributed) - thus bringing into play two vital, and politically significant, factors. First - despite the fact that it largely negates the arguments put forward around local democracy - the Government has taken powers to cap the level of local tax that may be set. Ten councils were capped for 1992/93; more were in previous years. This forces cuts in the council's budget and, therefore services, to meet the Government's limit. In addition, the fact that the criteria for capping are known in advance forces similar cuts in the budgets of many more councils in order to avoid being capped. Second, the fact that any gap between the levels of spending judged necessary by the Government and by the council can be bridged only through the local tax puts a dramatic 'ratchet', or 'gearing', effect on this charge. A simple example illustrates the point.

Let us take a hypothetical example of a council for which the Government had set the SSA at £100 million; its NNDR contribution is £40 million and the Government expects it to raise £15 million through local tax, leaving a Revenue Support Grant settlement of £45 million. But supposing the council's budget to maintain existing services were £115 million, it would have a gap of £15 million - which it could only raise by doubling the amount the Government expected it to raise in local tax (which would certainly lead to capping). In other words, a fifteen per cent increase in expenditure would lead to an increase in local tax of one hundred per cent, a ratchet factor of almost seven - which is more or less exactly the present situation. Even if the council were to cut services by £10 million (8.6 per cent), leaving just a five per cent rise in spending, it would have to raise the extra £5 million through local tax - making it thirty-three per cent higher than the level at which the Government says the council should set it (which would also lead to capping).

This example is illustrative rather than real, but there are many councils operating - or trying to - with problems on a scale not too dissimilar from those in the example. The political consequences of either large rises in local taxes or large cuts in local services are never far from councillors' minds. Yet, as can be clearly seen, it is central government that has its hands on the control levers. Since education accounts for around half the expenditure of most councils which are LEAs, any cuts are bound to affect the education service.

Conversely, if SSA is above the level of expenditure for a particular council, the effect is to reduce the local tax. The 'other services' SSA in 1990-91 for Westminster City Council (a key Conservative authority with a number of marginal wards, the loss of which in the 1990 elections would have given Labour control) was £68.77 million, but the council's expenditure on those services was only £28.11m. As John Austin-Walker MP said in the House of Commons: 'the difference between Westminster's SSA for "other services" and its actual expenditure represents a gift to the poll tax payers of Westminster of £301.17 each.' (*Hansard*, 24.6.92)

Many people are puzzled by the apparent contradiction between the determined pressure to reduce LEA spending on education, which we have outlined, and the Government's claim - with figures to prove it - that spending on education, which I have outlined, and the inflation), to record levels. (This is, of course, a somewhat shameless claim in the face of a clear policy objective to reduce public expenditure, but ministers - of any government - are never slow to take credit even where it isn't due.) Most people's experience, however, (in equally real terms) is of year-on-year cuts in provision. Several factors combine to provide an explanation for the fact that both the Government's claim and most people's experience are true. Briefly, the main ones are as follows:

inflation is measured by the Retail Price Index; education inflation is higher, so the 'real terms' adjustor is not actually real

wages and salaries - especially teachers' - have (quite rightly) risen faster than inflation in recent years, and the Government has not fully funded the cost to councils schools' needs have changed over the years, and computers (for example) cost more than paper and pencils

the Government's claim is based on spending *per pupil*, but there has been a large drop in pupil numbers - leading to a rise in unit costs

The measure that really matters is not how much is being spent, but how much it buys. It may be true that spending per pupil, adjusted by the Retail Price Index-based deflator, is at record levels. It is certainly also true, however, that the pupil:teacher ratio is worsening; that the state of repair and maintenance of school buildings is deteriorating; that the range and depth of LEA services is reducing; that the list of 'extras' for which a charge is made is growing; that the levels of charges are increasing and that the contribution to schools from fund-raising activities by parents is becoming ever more significant. More money is plainly buying less schooling. As a proportion of the Gross Domestic Product (GDP), spending on education is about the same now as it was in 1979. Tony Travers, an expert in local government finance from the London School of Economics, showed in an article in the *Times Educational Supplement* that between 1979 and 1986 spending on education fell from 5.2 per cent of the GDP to 4.9 per cent, and its share of public expenditure also fell, from 12.2 per cent to 10.9 per cent.[5] Both figures were largely restored to their 1979 levels by 1991, but compared with our international economic competitors, Britain fares very badly.

According to Will Hutton of the *Guardian*, real education spending per capita in Britain, as calculated by the OECD, declined by 1.8 per cent per annum between 1980 and 1987, the latest date for which comparable statistics were available.[6] 'That was the worst result of the 19 countries recorded; and the most recent figures suggest there is little subsequent improvement.' Most of the countries in the survey showed an increase over that period, with Germany, Belgium and the United States increasing by more than 4 per cent. Capital expenditure on schools also declined greatly during the 1980s, leading to the comment in 1989 from HMI that 'The state of secondary school buildings is a problem. HMI judged two-thirds of the schools inspected to have unsuitable accommodation and in just less than half of those the problems were serious and adversely affecting the quality of the work.'[7]

Having looked at the problem of LMS being introduced against a background of resources that are stretched increasingly thinly, let us turn to some of those inherent in the system itself.

There is now a major mismatch between power and responsibility over employment matters. Governing bodies have most of the powers of an employer, but not the responsibilities of being one, since the LEA remains the actual employer. They are able not only to hire but to 'fire' staff but, provided that they do not behave rashly - ignoring, or failing to take, sound advice - they are unlikely to have to bear the costs associated with redundancy or even unfair dismissal. LEAs are employers, but now have few of the powers to enable them to properly and fully exercise their responsibilities. This is one problem that GM status actually does resolve!

But perhaps the most striking, and best publicised problem is the effect of staff salaries on school budgets. Teachers gain increments on their salary scale for each year of experience, until they reach the top of the scale. Thus a school with a stable, experienced staff of teachers, most or many of whom will be at the top of the salary scale, will have a higher salary bill than a school with the same number of teachers that includes many who have recently qualified, and are thus still much lower down the scale. The difference could be quite substantial. Under LMS, the total teachers' salary cost as a component of the LEA's schools budget is calculated for the whole authority - based, obviously, on the actual level of salaries. That money is then distributed to schools through the formula - on the basis of the average salary cost in the authority. The school with staff at the top of the salary scales becomes a 'loser', whilst that with the inexperienced 'cheaper' teachers becomes a 'gainer'.

When the Government's proposals for LMS were first published, many believed this aspect of the arrangements to have been an error - but it was not. Some LEAs refused to accept it and built different provisions into their LMS schemes - which were subsequently rejected by the Secretary of State. It is the Government's (declared) intention that schools should have a choice between spending their budget on fewer 'expensive' teachers or more 'cheap' ones. The obvious problem with this - to which there is no obvious solution, other than some short-term help from transitional funding, under present requirements - is that schools are not setting up from scratch; they already have teachers, who have to be paid their correct *actual* salaries.

The effect of this situation on teacher morale is very damaging, particularly in areas - and times - when school spending is being cut. Experienced, 'expensive' teachers fear (justifiably) that schools will be reluctant to appoint them to vacancies; indeed, they feel vulnerable to replacement by 'cheaper' colleagues if their school has a budget crisis (severance costs being a charge on the LEA's budget, not the school's). Schools that do find themselves without enough in their budget to pay their current staff often look at opting out as a possible solution, thinking that they can spend some of the 'extra' money they will get in their budgets to cover the shortfall. The trouble is, it can only provide a temporary solution, especially if the extra money is short-lived. Diverting funds from other areas to staff salaries also diverts attention from the underlying cause of the problem. When it re-surfaces, it will have to be tackled properly; in the meantime, some aspects of provision, starved of funds and support, will have deteriorated badly - or disappeared.

There are many factors that can affect staff turnover. A socially advantaged school may have a stable staff because perhaps the job of the teacher is less demanding; housing and/or transport may be better and life is less of a struggle. Conversely, a less advantaged school, where these factors are reversed, may have a higher staff turnover, but will have considerably greater needs - including, surely, the need to attract and retain experienced teachers. Staff turnover may also reflect the style and quality of management within a school: a high turnover may result from poor relationships; a low turnover may reflect poor staff development, with fewer staff leaving for promotion. Whatever system of finance is applied, it cannot be educationally sound to put schools into a position where staff are made to feel increasingly vulnerable as they become more experienced; neither can it be right for schools in difficult circumstances to have insufficient resources to attract experienced staff. There must surely be a better means of resolving these problems than the present system offers.

Another criticism of the requirements imposed on LMS schemes is that the proportion of the budget that can be allocated according to need - now a maximum of twenty per cent - is not sufficient to reflect the different circumstances of schools within an authority, which may be quite extreme. There are many LEAs which include schools serving predominantly middle-class areas with few social problems and high levels of parental support for pupils, and others serving very disadvantaged communities; schools serving inner-city areas, suburbs and scattered rural communities; schools in modern buildings and others in old, often dilapidated buildings; schools on single sites and others on two or more sites; large schools and very small schools. The differences in the resources necessary to provide an equivalent service to the pupils in all these situations are often greater than the present system permits.

This problem is compounded by the fact that the increasing number of items in the LEAs' budgets that are now delegated to schools are subject to the age-weighting factor, despite the obvious fact that, for many, this is completely inappropriate. Heating costs and repairs and maintenance, for example, are likely to be at least as high (if not higher) per pupil in a small primary school than in a large secondary school; neither will they necessarily be lower in a secondary school without a sixth-form than in one with a sixth-form - yet, due to the age-weighting factor, a secondary school will receive more per pupil even for these items than a primary school, and a school with sixth-formers will receive more than one without.

So long as these deficiencies remain, the whole system works against a school that is struggling with problems, and favours the already advantaged. Yet a great many pupils will inevitably have their life chances largely determined in the former. The combination of formula funding (where each pupil has a cash value to a school) and open enrolment (where admission levels are restricted only by the capacity of schools) creates, in effect, a 'voucher' scheme within the state sector. Popular schools will flourish (relatively), whilst less popular schools - and their pupils - will be threatened with the spiral of decline described earlier. The distinctions between schools are likely to grow, and a two-tier system is likely to develop.

It is all very well to argue that, in theory, the same opportunities exist for all - but, in practice, they do not. Choice, wherever it exists, is only as real as people's means and ability to exercise it: the option of moving into the catchment area of a 'good' school is not open to many; those without cars find travelling more difficult; and many people have such problems to contend with that they are not in a position to do more than get their children to the nearest school. Most parents want the best for their children; those who are not, for whatever reason, able to choose it cannot just be written off as a feckless minority. Even if they were to be so, can there be any justification for denying young children the start in life that they deserve? To do so simply perpetuates and, to a large extent, exacerbates social divisions.

Education is a vital key to social and economic development, for both individuals and society generally. Equality of opportunity, a concept most people claim to support, is not delivered by equality of provision - and is obviously reversed by giving more to the already advantaged. It is frequently argued that 'throwing money at problems' is not the right solution, but where and how are the children of those that promote such views usually educated? Whilst money alone certainly cannot provide solutions, the provision of extra resources in school for those that lack opportunities at home, or have other disadvantages to overcome, has been clearly demonstrated to produce effective benefits, as the Plowden Report argued so successfully twenty-five years ago.

The forces of the market always favour the advantaged, those who have greatest 'purchasing' power. The dangers in allowing the provision of education to become even more subject than it has always been to such forces are obvious. If education, in its many complex aspects, is to be treated as simply a commodity available for 'purchase' (even if the state is providing the bulk of the funds) then those already best placed to take advantage of the offer will enhance their position further. The result is that society becomes increasingly unequal and divided, with consequences that have been seen around the world - and, as this is being written, are being seen again in our own cities: young people, with little share in the general affluence of the nation, and little prospect of honestly acquiring a share, behaving in a destructive, anti-social manner and attacking the possessions (and authority) of the rest of society.

In the next chapter we shall look at the background to these changes to the school system, particularly opting out, and examine their origins, the intention behind them and their initial reception. We shall then move on to look at what has happened during the first four years of opting out before going on to consider the implications of a major extension of the policy and its effect on choice in the school service.

NOTES

1 *The Educational System of England and Wales*, DES/Welsh Office, 1985 edition.
2 *The Education of the Adolescent*, Consultative Committee of the Board of Education, 1926.
3 *Secondary Education with Special Reference to Grammar Schools and Technical High Schools*, Consultative Committee of the Board of Education, 1938.
4 *Fifth Report*, Education, Science and Arts Committee, HMSO, 1991.
5 'Up, down and back to square one', *TES*, 3.4.92
6 *Guardian*, 27.1.92.
7 *Standards in Education 1988-89*, The Annual Report of HM Senior Chief Inspector of Schools.

3
THE POLITICAL BACKGROUND TO OPTING OUT

> The row ... arose from differences in the way (the plan to allow schools to opt out) was presented by Mrs Thatcher and Kenneth Baker, her Education Secretary ... The whole episode suggested that the Conservatives were .. 'making policy on the hoof'. This may be uncomfortably close to the truth because the plans originated within the closed circle of Conservative advisers on the right who have Mrs Thatcher's ear ... What has come out in the manifesto is clearly only the first instalment of a privatisation plan with far-reaching implications. (Stuart Maclure, editor of the *TES* writing in the *Sunday Times*, 31 May 1987.)

Policy formation of a political party is usually the result of a process combining ideological commitment, perceptions of public opinion and control or influence over the decision-making 'machinery' of the party. Apart from outside bodies, ministers usually have their own policy advisers, separate from their traditional civil service staff. In addition, the Downing Street policy unit has been increasingly involved in departmental policy in recent years (sometimes causing a degree of internal friction). Policy formation, then, is often in the hands of a small number of individuals, and it is this combination of factors that brought about opting out, and many of the other changes in the Education Reform Act 1988.

In a worsening national economic situation in the 1970s, there was growing public concern about the output of the education system, specifically of secondary schools. The then (Labour) Prime Minister, James Callaghan, made a speech at Ruskin College, Oxford in October 1976 which has since been widely regarded as the starting point of a 'Great Debate' on education - which is still going on. In fact, there has been some level of public and political debate, based on dissatisfaction with aspects of the education service, virtually since the introduction of universal education by the 1870 Act. The points most frequently at issue are the extent to which schools provide an education that satisfies the needs of the national economy, an issue beyond the scope of this book, and whether standards are rising or falling. This has meant that improving the education service, particularly in schools, has been seen as an important part of any would-be government's policy.

Throughout the 1970s and 1980s a variety of opinion formers on the Right and Left published reports, pamphlets and books criticising (or defending) schools, teachers, the system - and each other's ideas. By the time Kenneth Baker took over from Sir Keith Joseph as Secretary of State for Education in 1986, education was a major electoral issue. The Prime Minister, Margaret Thatcher, had herself been Education Secretary from 1970 to 1974 and was taking a keen interest in the subject. In an interview with Sir David English she said, 'We are going much further with education than we ever thought of doing before.'[1]

Mrs Thatcher's government was heavily influenced by the 'New Right', of which she was the undisputed leader. This led to a government programme of sweeping change, covering most public service areas, and causing differences of opinion within the Government and the Conservative Party. This was partly because of the break from the more old fashioned Toryism, but also because the range of new policy proposals was such that not all of the changes were properly considered even within government circles. Many of the more radical proposals sprang from ideological commitment rather than research. Opting out was certainly a source of controversy.

The groups proposing radical policy reform included the Centre for Policy Studies, the Adam Smith Institute, the Institute of Economic Affairs and the Hillgate Group. Several names crop up regularly from these groups, forming an influential - but not widely recognised - core network of approximately a dozen individuals. Most of the reforms of the 1988 Act have their roots in the publications of these few, although the Government was far more circumspect in the language it used to describe and explain its proposals than some of the original authors had been, as can be seen from the following examples:

> The second reason for enhancing parental choice, the first being the moral right to it, is a very practical one, that of the market. A 'market' in the true sense of the word is the interplay between supply and demand, between the providers of a good or service and the consumers of that good or that service. Whilst the popular conception of a market may be restricted to the buying and selling of goods, be it vegetables or motor cars, clearly a market can apply, and should apply, to services as well, indeed to anything which one group of people seeks to supply to another group of people who seek to consume. One such service is education.[2]

> If the system itself were changed to one of self-governing, self-managing, budget centres, which were obliged, for their survival, to respond to the 'market', then there would be an in-built mechanism to raise standards and change forms and types of education in accordance with the market demand.[3]

> Schools will have to work in order to stay in business, and the worse their results, the more likely they will be to go to the wall.[4]

Although the Government was not so blatant in its espousal of the market, there was no disguising the radical nature of the proposed reforms - nor where they were targeted - which, inevitably, provoked widespread interest in the run-up to the general election in June 1987:

> Thousands of schools could be 'privatised' under a plan now being proposed for inclusion in the Conservative Party election manifesto. The scheme, which has influential backers, would be the most radical of a series of policies designed to shake up the education service.
> (*Sunday Telegraph*, 26 April 1987)

A revolutionary plan to free schools from the shackles of Left-wing councils is to be the major plank of a 'consumer-is-king' Tory election manifesto. Schools will be allowed to opt out of local authority control and be funded directly from Whitehall. And parents will be able to choose any school they like as a free-market system replaces 'catchment area' limitations.
(*Mail on Sunday*, 26 April 1987)

Mr Baker said he believed that 'a large number of schools' - particularly in the inner cities - would take the opportunity to free themselves from council interference.
(*Daily Telegraph*, 20 May 1987)

Head teachers, who play the central role in the Tory party manifesto proposals for breaking up the comprehensive system, will not want to take their schools out of local authority control, Mr David Hart, general-secretary of the National Association of Head Teachers, said yesterday ... Mr Hart said: 'Quite honestly, for all the faults of local education authorities - and we have criticised them ourselves in the past for their bureaucracy and tendency to interfere excessively in schools - we cannot really go along with the concept the Conservatives have put forward. Why the Government cannot give support to the need to improve the system that we have at the present time, and why it has to go for this extremely radical solution, which I don't think, quite frankly, will create the improvement in standards they think it will, is beyond belief.
(*Guardian*, 20 May 1987)

Mrs Thatcher indicated yesterday that the Conservative Party's radical plans for reforming State schooling could lead to the return of a selective education system. Schools which decided to break away from the control of local education authorities would be allowed to select their own pupils, possibly by a written exam, she said ... But Mr Baker, Education Secretary, who was not on the platform when Mrs Thatcher made her comments, later denied that the 11-plus would be restored. He said: 'What happens today is that if a popular school is oversubscribed, the head teacher has to engage in a selection process. The head will look at the pupil's record and probably interview them and have some aptitude tests. We would expect that sort of process to

continue.[5]
(*Daily Telegraph*, 23 May 1987)

> Mrs Thatcher's opponents proclaim that the Conservative Party is now in the embarrassing position of having two contradictory policies on education, which is supposed to be one of the most important issues before the electorate. The Prime Minister ... wants to re-introduce selection. Mr Baker does not. Thus a national debate which everyone was encouraged to believe had been settled, for good or ill, more than 20 years ago has suddenly been reopened bizarrely and unexpectedly. It prompts many questions, in addition to the fundamental one of whether selection is desirable, such as: why is it not in the manifesto? And: is it a vote winner? ... The pity is that instead of grasping this historic nettle, Conservative leaders - but not the bolder, more candid Mrs Thatcher - show every sign of blindly falling over it. The middle of an election campaign may not be the best time to be making policy. But the confusion that has been created by the contradictory signals emanating from Mrs Thatcher and Mr Baker must be quickly dispelled and replaced by a clear commitment.
> (Leader in *The Times*, 26 May 1987)

(Five years later, there has still been no such clear commitment. Indeed, the situation is now even less clear, as it is known that GM schools may apply to become selective but the criteria by which the Secretary of State will decide such applications are not known. Also, the new emphasis on specialisation in schools seems bound to lead to the introduction of more widespread, if different forms of, selection.)

> Head teachers fear that Conservative Party plans to allow schools to break away from local education authority control will lead to the dismemberment of the education service. David Hart ... said yesterday that his members were deeply suspicious that the Conservatives were intent on 'dismantling the education system by the back door.'
> (*Independent*, 30 May 1987)

Following the 1987 election, a series of consultation papers were published in July, with responses required by

September - the worst possible part of the year for schools, and those involved with them, to react. As Ngaio Crequer commented in the *Independent* (6 August 1987), 'A week may be a long time in politics, but nine weeks over the summer break is no time at all in education ... You could be a die-hard opponent of Mr Baker's reforms, you could be a staunch supporter ... or you could be, as we think many are, perhaps the majority: confused, uncertain, lacking knowledge, prepared for some quite radical changes but wanting to think hard about, discuss and test what is proposed.' Nevertheless, around 16,500 (mostly hostile) responses were submitted. A flavour of the opposition to the opting out clauses can be found in the following examples:

> The question must be ... asked as to whether there are additional objectives being served by the proposal, to do with relations between national and local government. It is quite clear that the effect of large scale adoption of GM status will weaken the position of local government in a fundamental way. This is a development which we would not find acceptable. We see the maintaining of strong (and responsible) local government as an essential element in the future of democracy in this country and, even if we did not, we would still deplore the use of the education system as a pawn in what was essentially a political intention. (Chairman, Board of Education, General Synod of the Church of England)

> Schools are community assets paid for out of community rates and used by adults and children alike. To allow a minority of parents passing through a school to take the school out of local authority support is totally at odds with the desire to give more power and greater choice to all parents.
> (Advisory Centre for Education (ACE))

> We are forced to conclude that the proposals for GM schools will damage rather than improve state education. These proposals must be resisted by those who are concerned about the majority of the pupils within state education. (The National Confederation of Parent-Teacher Associations)

> Governors of GM schools will indeed be asked to take on many
> responsibilities and will be responsible for the way in which
> educational resources, provided by the whole community, will be
> spent in one school. It is not clear to whom these governing
> bodies will be accountable, or by whom they will be appointed ...
> If these schools are to be the direct responsibility of the Secretary
> of State, it is difficult to see what practical say the community will
> have. (The National Association of Governors and Managers (NAGM))

The most embarrassing source of objections was parents, in
whose name opting out was allegedly being introduced.
The *Daily Telegraph* (24 August 1987) reported:

> Major educational reforms aimed at giving parents more influence
> and a wider choice of schools face rejection from the very people
> the Government hopes will benefit most. All three leading
> national parents' groups are preparing responses which are
> believed to be highly critical of the reforms. They will tell
> Mr Baker, Education Secretary, that 'opting out' and allowing
> popular schools to expand will not work. The opposition from
> the organised parents' lobby is bound to prove an embarrassment
> to the Government, which has always held that most parents would
> welcome a greater say in schools. But Mr Baker is likely to argue
> that the parents' groups are unrepresentative of parents as a whole.

The Great Education Reform Bill (as Mr Baker called it, or
GERBIL, as it became known) was published in November
1987. To nobody's great surprise, its proposals varied little
from those of the White Paper - despite the responses.
It completed its parliamentary stages during the spring
and summer, in the face of vigorous opposition to some
measures. Hindsight offers an interesting perspective on the
debate on opting out, the nature of which is illustrated by
the quotations which follow from the Bill's second reading
in the House of Commons.[6] Many of the issues raised are
those that still need careful consideration today.

Kenneth Baker, moving the second reading, explained
the Government's thinking behind the reforms:

> Raising the quality of education in our schools is the most
> important task facing this Parliament. Both the Prime Minister and

56

I have made that clear...

Our education system has operated over the past 40 years on the basis of the framework laid down by Rab Butler's 1944 Act ... We need to inject a new vitality into that system. It has become producer-dominated ... There is now a growing realisation that radical change is necessary ...

Our proposals will allow ... schools to opt out of local authority control and to apply for direct funding. This will widen choice for many parents in the state-maintained sector for whom all too often the only choice is to take it or leave it. This wider choice will help improve standards in all schools, not just those which opt out. The LEAs will want to hold on to their schools and will, therefore, have a far greater incentive to respond to the wishes of parents. For the first time in 80 years they will face competition in the provision of free education, so standards will rise in all schools as we introduce a competitive spirit into the provision of education - and at no extra cost to the consumer.

Meanwhile, let me stress and make clear that these schools will offer free education. They will be funded at the same level as they would have been had they remained under their local authority. There will be an equality of public resourcing. The detailed procedures set out in this Bill ensure that opting out will be an open, democratic process.

Jack Straw, responding for Labour, made it clear that, whilst he shared the concern over the quality of education, he fundamentally disagreed with the measures proposed. His particular concerns were the degree of centralisation of power and the dangers in a market-led system:

There is no question more important than the education of the nation's children, but the Bill will severely damage that education. From beginning to end the Bill is based upon a deception. Its very title - "Education Reform Bill" - is a fraud; it should be called the "Education (State Control) Bill". Under the disguise of fine phrases like "parental choice" and "decentralisation" the Bill will deny choice and instead centralise power and control over schools ... in the hands of the Secretary of State in a manner without parallel in the western world.

(Rab) Butler recognised that it was only through equality of opportunity that talents could flower, that richness and diversity in our national life could occur, that individuals could be fulfilled and that one nation could be created. Butler spoke directly of egalitarianism. It is that which the Secretary of State now wishes to destroy. As he told the Tory party conference: 'The pursuit of egalitarianism is over.' ... Opting out will be a fraud. Yes, schools will be able to opt out of locally led education, but they will opt into not independence but state control of a direct and authoritarian kind. The Secretary of State will have direct control of these schools, including the power to close them. The local authority will have no power, only the duty to pay for them. We do not need to muse about where the proposals will lead. We have the proposals' authors, the Hillgate group, the Institute of Economic Affairs and the "no turning back" group of Conservative Back Benchers who want to replace the right to a free education with a giro or a voucher to help pay towards some part of children's education while parents have to pay towards the rest. The proposals for per capita funding, for open admissions and for opting out take us straight down that road. The authors want an unregulated market in education.

Edward Heath, in a contribution that attracted a great deal of public attention, attacked the opting out proposals in particular for the damage they would do to the system of school provision, and to the education of many children. The hostility towards LEAs from a number of Conservative MPs was apparent during his speech:

> I wish to deal with the vital question of opting out, because it destroys the system that was built up by Disraeli, Balfour and Butler. One of my hon. Friends on the Benches behind me said, in an intervention, that opting out represents the choice between freedom and not opting out. That implies that to remain in a local education authority is a form of tyranny. (Hon. Members: 'It is') Well, there it is. That reveals the real attitude of some of my hon. Friends behind me ... I hear the cry 'Look at (X)' and that gets us to the point. We are going through the whole of this process because of the madness of (X and Y)[7] and two or three others out of more than 100 education authorities. That is what it is all about. What will happen as a consequence? We shall see that schools will opt out. The next development will be that those

schools can choose whom they take. They will not take from their area, but take the bright pupils wherever they find them. The next stage will be 'Yes you can charge fees for doing that'. We will move right away from our educational system to a fee-paying system of independent schools of choice ... Well, the Secretary of State may shake his head, but he knows perfectly well that that is the philosophy behind this whole process. It is immensely damaging to the education system of this country. It will be divisive and it will be fatal to the education of a large number of children ... Opting out should be dropped completely. It will undermine the whole of the basic educational system of this country.

Paddy Ashdown concentrated on the likely effects on parental choice, and what he saw as the Government's determination to re-introduce selection in schools:

Choice, improved standards and the removal of politics from education are the three aims of the Bill as stated by the Secretary of State, and they are aims with which we entirely agree. Governments, however - particularly the present Government - should not be judged by their rhetoric. The question before us now is whether the Bill will achieve those aims. The resounding answer, as expressed by the thousands of responses to the consultation paper, is no. While there is no doubt that the Bill will provide choice for some, for many it will provide only a form of entrapment. Another secret item on the Government's agenda is the unscrupulous, undercover and unacceptable re-introduction of selective education. Of course, the Secretary of State does not admit as much, but his junior Ministers and the Prime Minister herself have been somewhat more frank and blunt. The effect of the opting-out proposals, the fact that they are irreversible and the ease with which a school's character can be changed will inevitably and inexorably take us back to the days of a divided education system and the discarding of children at the age of 11.

Michael Heseltine warned of the problems opting out could pose to the rationalisation of schools that was required if resources were to be properly directed towards improving standards:

The first proposal which I would like to discuss with my right hon. Friend is that of opting out. No one pretends - certainly not

my right hon. Friend - that he can foresee the pace at which individual decisions to opt out will be made ... it is obvious that in many parts of the country the right to opt out will coincide with a substantial fall in the number of children in our schools ...
To manage that scale of reduction and achieve value for money in the education programme, it must follow that very significant reductions in the number of schools must take place. The worst outcome would be to run our educational system within buildings that are only half or two-thirds used. That is not only the worst way to raise the quality of education, but as the Audit Commission has said, it perpetuates an annual waste of the best part of £750 million because we are not getting value for money out of the existing education budget. No hon. Member of whatever party can afford to ignore wasted expenditure of the tune of £750 million a year if he is seeking to improve education standards.

By the time the Bill reached the House of Lords, it had grown from 137 clauses to 198 as the result of amendments tabled by the Government and passed by the House of Commons - where debate had been severely curtailed by the imposition of a 'guillotine', and where the Government had a majority of over one hundred. In the Lords, however, the Government suffered a severe defeat over the ballot procedure for opting out: an amendment moved by the Bishop of London was passed (with a majority of nineteen) requiring not just a simple majority of parents voting to support opting out, but a majority of those eligible to vote. In due course, the Government conceded a compromise and introduced provision for a second ballot to be held if the turnout in the first was below fifty per cent. (The details of opt out procedures are described in Chapter 7.)

The Bill received the Royal Assent on 29 July 1988, becoming the Education Reform Act.

In order to promote the policy of opting out, the Grant-Maintained Schools Trust was established in August 1988 - with a number of Conservative Party activists at its heart. As the *TES* reported:

> The trust is the independent, privately-funded body launched last month to advise heads, governors and parents on the pros and cons of opting out. It is run by Andrew Turner, a former researcher at Tory Central Office and Steve Norris, the affable former Conservative MP for Oxford East.[8]

(It should be noted that Andrew Turner is also a Conservative Oxford City Councillor.) In a glossy brochure sent to schools, the Trust claimed that 'As a registered charity it is independent of, but fully briefed by, the Department of Education and Science and is able to provide advice and assistance free of charge to schools preparing for grant-maintained status'. In fact, the Trust was not a charity, which caused a major political row, and an embarrassing withdrawal of the claim. As the *TES* also noted:

> The 'independent of the DES' bit should be taken with a pinch of salt. It is so independent that the trust chairman, Steve Norris, was asked by Mr Baker to take on the job.

The Secretary of State also made clear that if the Trust were to apply to his department for financial assistance towards specific activities intended to provide assistance to schools which had acquired GM status, 'the department would be prepared to consider it'. A separate organisation, Choice in Education was set up, with Andrew Turner as Director and funding from individuals and companies, as the campaigning arm - though the two have continued to share a common (London) office address and phone number. The Education Department has funded the Trust ever since, with £25,000 in 1988-89; £250,000 in 1989-90; £448,000 in 1990-91 and £600,000 in 1991-92 (by the end of which there were still only 219 GM schools). In the meantime, the Grant Maintained Schools Foundation, which does have charitable status, was established. Robert Balchin, another well-known Conservative, chairs the Foundation, the Trust and Choice.

Local Schools Information was established in May 1989

to provide an alternative source of information on opting out. Set up initially for one year, LSI is still going three years later and is now funded by about half the LEAs in the country - right across the political spectrum. LSI has continued to be the main alternative source of information on the issue to the organisations described above, and the DFE - which has itself produced a range of (sometimes controversial) booklets on the subject, and distributed well over a million copies of them to schools, at taxpayers' expense.

The origins of the policy of opting out have not been a major concern of those interested in the position of their own school, who are, naturally, more interested in its immediate (and possibly future) practical implications. However, as we shall see in Chapter 9, there is a strong link between the objectives of the policy and the practical implications for schools. Next, however, we shall look at how opting out got under way, and its progress over the four years during which it has been an option for schools.

OPTING OUT FROM 1988 TO 1992

It seemed likely, and indeed became the case, that the first few (but only very few) schools to opt out would receive widespread national publicity, bringing unique opportunities to attract financial sponsorship from business and commercial interests. Whilst there has continued to be a high level of local press coverage of schools opting out, especially of the first ones in a particular area, there is now little apparent interest in sponsorship. It is only controversial cases which have attracted the kind of attention that was given to the race to become the first grant-maintained school, which actually ended in a dead- heat.

The ballots at Skegness Grammar School, Lincolnshire and St James' Church of England Comprehensive, Bolton both closed on 2 November 1988; the ballot at Audenshaw

High School, Tameside closed on 5 December. All three had turnouts of over eighty per cent, with more than ninety per cent of voters supporting opting out (99.6 per cent voted 'Yes' at St James', which was facing closure). The decision on St James' School was delayed by the need to consider the LEA's conflicting proposal to close the school, so the first two schools to be given GM status by the Secretary of State were Skegness and Audenshaw, in an announcement on 22 February 1989. *The Times* reported the Secretary of State as saying:

> These two schools have been bold enough to grasp the opportunity to control their own destinies. They have been quick to see the advantages of their new freedom.

The news appeared in *Today* under the headline 'And now a lesson from our sponsor'.

A total of twelve schools held ballots during the autumn term of 1988, ten of which voted in favour of opting out and two against. The spring term of 1989 saw ballots in a further thirty-one schools, eleven of which voted against the idea - seven of them with more than seventy-five per cent of 'No' votes. By the end of the school year in July 1989, 55 schools had held ballots on opting out, and 40 had voted in favour of GM status (11 of which were subsequently rejected by the Secretary of State); 15 had opted not to opt out.

The first eighteen schools to become grant-maintained did so with effect from September 1989. They were joined in January 1990 by two more, and a further ten by the end of the school year; a total of thirty - out of over seven thousand five hundred eligible secondary and primary schools (primary schools with fewer than three hundred pupils were not originally eligible). Despite the earlier assurances of Kenneth Baker that opting out would not be a lifeboat for schools facing closure, no fewer than fourteen of the thirty were in just that position, or facing some other unwelcome reorganisation plan. (Only twelve schools, all facing closure or reorganisation, had had their applications rejected.) This was obviously not the start that the government had hoped for.

Kenneth Baker suggested that one reason for the slow take-up was 'blatant intimidation' by LEAs, and on 13 February 1989 he issued a code of practice, including 'new ministerial powers to order a new vote where councils are judged to have pressured schools to stay within the local education authority'.[9] Neil Fletcher, chair of the Association of Metropolitan Authorities Education Committee, was quoted on the same day as saying: 'These allegations are a smokescreen to cover Mr Baker's embarrassment at the failure of parents to respond to his grant-maintained schools gimmick' (*Daily Telegraph*); 'Had any local education authority acted improperly as he suggests, legal action would have been taken' (*Independent*); and 'Local authorities believe parents should have all the facts before them before they vote. When we put information before parents it is "distortion" but when he does it, it is "informing the parents"' (*Guardian*). Interestingly, no ballot has ever been re-run on this account nor, so far as the author is aware, has any action been taken against any LEA. In response to this low take-up of GM status, the Government decided to offer additional inducements. At the Conservative Party conference in October 1990, the (then) Secretary of State, John MacGregor, announced dramatic increases in the grants to GM schools and the removal of the size limit on primary schools (although, by then, not a single primary school, even amongst the larger ones, had held a ballot), whilst simultaneously talking up the success of the policy. In his speech, Mr MacGregor said:

> Freedom and choice are flourishing in the accelerating number of Grant-Maintained Schools - the 'Jewel in the Crown' of parent power. This time last year we had eighteen - not bad for a flying start. Yesterday we had forty-eight. Today we have fifty ...

> GM schools have already proved their worth. So today I am
> announcing four more measures to build on this success ...

The maximum level of transitional grant was doubled (from
£30,000 to £60,000), whilst some special purpose grants
and the formula allocation of capital grant were increased
by fifty per cent (the details of grants to GM schools are
described in Chapter 6).

Throughout this period, the Department of Education
sent booklets on opting out[10] to all eligible schools and
reminded governors of the policy through their termly
newsletter. Education ministers made few speeches, and
gave few interviews, without including a passage on opting
out, generally in terms of the great success of the policy.
Media interest in the issue remained at a fairly high
level, and some newspapers ran regular items on the
advantages that opting out was bringing to featured schools
- often accompanied by highly critical references to local
authorities.

The greater inducements and relentless promotion had
some effect. During the school year from September 1990 to
July 1991, 204 schools held ballots, with 162 voting to opt
out and 42 voting not to.

Early ballots were spread across a wide range of LEAs,
the forty-three held during the first two terms covering
thirty LEAs. Kenneth Baker, in a speech at the Young
Conservatives Conference on 12 February 1989 said:

> As for parents' abilities to take decisions on opting out, the proof
> of the pudding is in the voting. So far 28 ballots have taken
> place. 25 more are in the pipeline. In those ballots we have
> had so far the average turnout has been 73%. In 11 ballots the
> turnout has been over 80% - a staggering figure. It shows just
> how interested parents are when given the chance to decide on
> the future of their children's school. And we have seen several
> massive majorities in favour of schools opting out of the LEA and
> seeking grant-maintained status. This is parent power in action.
> We have also seen parents vote against opting out. In Bromley,

Sussex, Trafford and Kent moves to opt out were rejected. Well that too is parental choice. I note that in these 4 cases parents were giving an overwhelming vote of confidence to Conservative-controlled LEAs!

As more schools held ballots, several patterns began to emerge - some of which ran counter to the impression created by government claims. An analysis by Local Schools Information of the 428 ballots held by 31 January 1992 produced some interesting results.[11] Over half of the ballots were in only twelve of the 117 LEAs, whilst no ballots at all had been held in thirty-six. Thus, rather than spreading across the country, opting out was becoming concentrated in a small handful of areas - a trend that has continued beyond the general election. By the end of July 1992, there were no more than nineteen LEAs where the number of ballots was in double figures, accounting between them for two-thirds of all the ballots, whilst thirty-two had still not experienced a single ballot. 244 schools had voted to opt out in county authorities, compared with 87 in metropolitan areas, and 13.2 per cent of the secondary schools in Conservative-controlled LEAs had voted to opt out compared with 2.2 per cent in Labour authorities; both the number of ballots and the proportion in favour of opting out were higher in Conservative areas. The idea that opting out would appeal to parents anxious to escape Labour inner-city councils had plainly been wrong; and parents were apparently giving a vote of confidence to Labour, rather than Conservative, LEAs.

There was also a clear link with the level of spending on schools. Discounting the schools where the threat of reorganisation was an issue, of the remaining 204 English secondary schools which had voted to opt out, 103 were in the lowest spending twenty five LEAs whilst only twelve were in the highest spending twenty five.

In 45 per cent of the schools voting to opt out, fewer than half the eligible parents voted 'Yes'; in 31 per cent of these cases, the margin between those voting Yes:No was smaller than 60:40. A similar survey by Local Schools Information in July 1991 (based on the first 297 ballots) had shown the development of these trends, with one conspicuous difference: the proportion of schools voting to opt out where the margin between those in favour of opting out and those against was smaller than 60:40 almost doubled from 16 to 31 per cent. In other words, parents were evidently finding the issue increasingly contentious. Of the exactly 100 schools voting to opt out between the two surveys, the number resulting in a margin closer than 60:40 was 65 - a fourfold increase on the earlier proportion of just 16 per cent.

As the general election approached, opting out emerged as the major area of policy difference between the parties, with the Conservatives firmly committed to an extension of the GM sector and both the main opposition parties equally committed to ending opting out and restoring GM schools to their LEAs. It was important to the Government to make opting out appear as popular as possible so, almost at the last minute, they made great haste to bring the number of GM schools to over two hundred before the election.

On 1 April 1992, just eight days before the election, seventy-four more schools in England were given grant-maintained status, bringing the total from just one hundred and forty-three to over two hundred. The number opting out on that date came as quite a surprise to observers and, probably, to many in the schools concerned; especially since, had there been a change of government, these late additions would barely have had time to change the sign outside the school before the process began to bring them back within their LEAs.

Just how this was done starkly illustrates the manner, and haste, in which ministerial in-trays were cleared as the election approached. According to the Department of Education progress report on GM schools published on 10

February, the number of schools approved to opt out on 1 April was thirty-nine, with nine more 'minded to approve'. This would not have taken the total over two hundred. Between 3 February and 10 March, thirty-five schools, with a total of around twenty-two thousand pupils, were told that they would become grant-maintained on 1 April - giving them a transitional period (in which to sort out all the necessary arrangements for the change from being part of a LEA to being independent) of a maximum of eight weeks. In five cases, the transitional period was only four weeks and in another five, only three weeks. Such haste was unprecedented.

It also ignored the guidance given by the DES itself that 'to allow for an orderly transition to the new status' governors should publish their proposals by the end of the previous August if they wish to opt out from 1 April.[12] Only thirty-four of the seventy-four schools to opt out on 1 April 1992 had published their proposals by the end of August 1991; eleven had yet to do so by the end of November. Following publication, there is a statutory two-month period for objections to be sent to the Secretary of State, which he is bound to consider before he can make a decision (normally one to three months later). Several of this group were decided within a fortnight of the closure for objections, including The Beacon School, Surrey, which was singled out (from four decisions announced on 20 February) as the two-hundredth school to receive the Secretary of State's approval - giving Kenneth Clarke the perfect combination of symbolic name and photo opportunity.

There was obvious uncertainty about the future of opting out during this time and, not surprisingly, the number of ballots fell in the run-up to the election. Media interest in the issue was intense but, astonishingly, the opposition parties did not turn opting out - nor, indeed, education as a whole - into a major electoral issue. (In fact, far more attention was paid to the health care of Jennifer's ear than to the education of seven million pupils!)

In spite of all the Government's efforts, by the end of this period only a very small percentage of eligible schools had decided to opt for GM status. We shall return later to the position arising from the election result and consider the broader implications of the extension of opting out. First, we shall look in more detail at the situation as it affects the people involved in schools - governors, parents and staff - and then move on to the financial arrangements and procedures for opting out.

NOTES

1   *Daily Mail*, 1.5.1987.
2   *Opting to Grant Maintained Schools*, Stuart Sexton, Institute of Economic Affairs, 1989.
3   *Our Schools - A Radical Policy*, Stuart Sexton, Institute of Economic Affairs, 1987.
4   *Whose Schools? A Radical Manifesto,* The Hillgate Group, 1986.
5   Mr Baker was not actually correct. It is normally the LEA, not heads, who undertake this task, using the authority's (objective) criteria as published in its admissions policy.
6   *Hansard*, 1.12.87.
7   'X' and 'Y': two LEAs that were widely tagged as 'Loony Left' by Conservative MPs at the time.
8   *TES*, 16.8.88.
9   *Independent*, 13.2.89.
10 *How to Become a Grant-Maintained School*, first edition 1988, and *Grant-Maintained Schools: Questions Parents ask*, DFE, first edition 1990.
11 *Opting Out 1988 - 1992*, Local Schools Information, February 1992.
12 *How to Become a Grant-Maintained School,* DES, first edition 1988.

4

GOVERNORS AND PARENTS

GOVERNORS

We have already covered briefly the composition and responsibilities of the governing bodies of GM schools. Here we shall look at the situation in LEA-maintained schools before returning in more detail to the particular changes that arise as a result of opting out.

The Education (No.2) Act 1986 made a number of key changes to the way in which state schools were governed. According to a Department for Education leaflet:

> The 1986 Act establishes a new statutory framework for school government. The respective roles of the governors, the headteacher and the local authority are clearly defined in a way that enables each of them to make their own distinctive contribution to the school's success.[1]

The 1986 Act altered the composition and powers of the governing bodies of most schools, giving more places to parents and community representatives (the composition of those of Voluntary Aided schools was not affected). Its provisions were phased in over a period from 1987 to 1989 - in the middle of which the 1988 Act was passed, bringing LMS and the possibility of opting out. It has not been a dull time for governors, nor for those responsible for the administration of governing bodies.

The National Association of Governors and Managers (NAGM) welcomed the changes, saying:

> The 1986 Act has a lot to offer governors, especially in areas where they have been accepted only reluctantly, and given little encouragement to carry out their role effectively. We believe that the quality of staff appointments, curriculum policy and discipline

can be significantly enhanced by an effective, supportive governing body.

We saw in Chapter 1 the composition of the governing body of a GM school, which currently does not vary with the size of the school. The comparison with LEA county schools is as follows:

LEA schools:

No of pupils	up to 99	100-299	300-599	600 + *	GM schools
Parents**	2	3	4	5	5
Teachers**	1	1	2	2	1 or 2
LEA appointees	2	3	4	5	n/a***
Co-optees†	3	4	5	6	8 or 9 min***
Headteacher‡	1	1	1	1	1
Total	9	12	16	19	15 or 17 min

* These schools may adopt the composition for 300-599 pupils if preferred.

** These refer to the number of *elected* parent and teacher governors; GM schools have a choice between 1 and 2 teacher governors.

*** GM schools have first/foundation governors in place of these groups, at least two of whom must be parents at the time of their appointment.

† Voluntary controlled schools have 1 co-opted governor and the balance of this group are 'foundation' governors.

‡ Headteachers of LEA-maintained schools may choose whether to be a governor or not; in GM schools, they must be.

The governing body of voluntary aided (and special-agreement)[2] schools consists of: at least one elected parent; at least one LEA appointee; at least one elected teacher in schools with fewer than 300 pupils, and at least two for larger schools; at least one minor authority[3] appointee at a primary school serving an area with a minor authority; the headteacher if s/he chooses; a number of foundation governors sufficient to outnumber the non-foundation governors by two if the governing body has eighteen or fewer members and by three if it has more. At least one of

71

the foundation governors must be the parent of a child at the school at the time of their appointment.

Many schools have more parents on their governing bodies by including them in other categories as well as the elected group. Many also have a member of the non-teaching staff on the governing body through co-option; this is not possible in a GM school, where no member of the staff of the school can serve as a first governor. Thus the only way in which non-teaching staff can be governors of a GM school is if any are eligible, and successfully stand, for election as parent governors.

In 1978, the independent Taylor Committee's report (see page 80) recommended an equal share of places on governing bodies between parents, LEA, staff, and members of the local community.[4] As can be seen, the balance struck by the 1986 Act, whilst giving equal numbers to parents and LEA-appointees, offers significantly fewer places to staff (none to non-teaching staff) and more to 'the community' in the form of co-optees (who are nominated by the other governors). The co-opted governors (and the first governors of a GM school) must include a representative of the local business community. The LEA appointees are normally nominated by the local political parties, in proportions which broadly reflect the balance between the parties on the local authority.

Pupil governors, which were being introduced in secondary schools in some areas, are no longer permitted; nobody under eighteen may be a governor.

The 1986 Act made basic changes to the responsibilities of governing bodies, increasing and clarifying them. The additional changes, especially LMS, under the 1988 Act have made the governing body even more crucial to the success of a school, and the task of being a governor is now quite onerous - though rewarding.

All state schools have an Instrument and Articles of Government. These are statutory controls over, respectively, the conduct and the powers and responsibilities of the governing body. The Articles of Government of schools must provide for the general conduct of the school to be under the direction of the governing body. More specifically, governing bodies:

must produce a curriculum policy statement, taking account of that of the LEA, which must include the provisions of the National Curriculum and those for religious education and collective worship

must decide whether sex education should be provided at the school

may offer the headteacher general principles for a policy on discipline, and play a central part in the procedure for exclusion of pupils from school

must make information about the school available to parents and others (ie. publish a school booklet/prospectus), which must include details of exam results and other achievements

must prepare an annual report for parents and hold an annual meeting to discuss the report and other matters concerning their role in running the school

must decide a policy on charging for 'optional extras'

The LEA must publish its admissions arrangements annually for county schools and must first consult governing bodies on its implementation; it may not vary the arrangements without consultation.

In voluntary aided schools the governing bodies are also responsible for: the admissions policy; employing the staff; keeping the building in good repair.

These responsibilities existed before the additional demands (of financial and management responsibility) brought about by LMS (covered in Chapter 2).

GOVERNING BODIES OF GM SCHOOLS

We have covered most of the differences in the constitution and powers/responsibilities between the governing bodies of LEA-maintained and GM schools elsewhere. In summary, the additional responsibilities in GM schools resulting from the break with the LEA are as follows:

they become the employer of staff, and will be involved in all aspects of employment practice - of which they may have little experience

they are responsible for staff recruitment, including cover for vacancies and absences

they decide the school's admissions policy and handle parental appeals against non-admission or exclusion of pupils

they must make the necessary arrangements for the assessment and testing of pupils at the required ages

they must identify, and secure appropriate provision for, children with special educational needs (a responsibility shared with the LEA, despite opting out)

they must provide for the induction, in-service training and appraisal of teachers

they must comply with a number of statutory measures, including the Race and Sex Discrimination Acts; Health & Safety at Work Act and regulations on standards of school premises

they must manage the whole of the school's budget, and ensure provision of services the school requires that are no longer provided automatically by the LEA

They also need to buy in professional services for some purposes - including to advise them, should the need arise, on exercising the responsibilities listed above.

74

A number of schools, on opting out, have tried to include professional people such as accountants, architects or surveyors, lawyers and others as first governors, so that they have a variety of 'in-house' expertise. Whilst this may be very wise in some ways, such people - if they are successful - are likely to be very busy, and may have had little or no experience of school administration. Also, a governing body should reflect the community it serves, especially if it is through the governors that accountability is supposed to be exercised. Not many communities consist of a high proportion of such professionals.

It is appropriate to raise one major point about accountability here. The first governors are required to form a majority on the governing body, which then itself becomes responsible for filling any vacancies in that category. Their terms of office are between five and seven years (determined initially by the school's original governing body in the proposals for GM status); in contrast, elected governors' term of office is four years. Thus, appointed governors are in a powerful position compared with their elected colleagues, and it is hard to see how real accountability can be exercised; the potential for a self-perpetuating oligarchy is clear.

Despite the fact that GM schools are 'run entirely by their governors' (Parents' Charter) and that 'all decisions are taken by the governors (who include the headteacher)' (Department for Education booklet *How to Become a Grant-Maintained School*), there has been considerable pressure from headteachers of GM schools (described in Chapter 9) to curb their powers. A document of guidance to governors produced by the Department for Education[5] says:

> In order to perform the tasks required of them governors need to know generally how the school operates... Visits to the school can be a valuable source of information and can be used to perform other tasks ... When planning visits, governing

bodies must realise that the headteacher is given responsibility for running the school during the school day and that visits by governors will have an effect on the functioning of the school. Therefore, governors should seek the permission of the headteacher before undertaking visits.

Whilst, in any school, it is both sensible and common courtesy for governors to visit by mutual convenience and appointment, the use of the term 'permission' casts an interesting light on the respective roles of governor and head. In effect, those with responsibility for the school (and the employers of the head) must seek the permission of their manager (and employee) before visiting the school for which they are responsible - and, theoretically, accountable to parents.

THE POSITION OF PARENTS

A great many of the recent changes to the school system have been made for the expressed purpose of enhancing the position of parents, and increasing the influence they are able to bring on the education provided for their children. Grant-maintained schools were described by John MacGregor, when he was (briefly) Secretary of State for Education as 'the Jewel in the Crown of parent power'. However, 'parent power' is an ill-defined concept. As Margaret Morrissey, ex-President of the National Confederation of Parent Teacher Associations, put it: 'I must have talked to thousands and thousands of parents ... and I don't think I've spoken to one who has ever said they wanted parent power and who have not accepted that the school and the teachers are the professionals. And while they don't expect to be talked down to, they don't expect to go into schools and tell teachers how to do their job.'[6] It is the author's experience too, having also spoken to thousands of parents, that power is not what parents want. They want, above all, for their children to receive 'a good education', and for many that implies a better education than they received themselves.

Often parents do not feel confident that they know enough about exactly what 'a good education' is; they generally know whether or not their children are happy at school (which is very important) and have a sense - but probably not enough detailed knowledge - of whether or not they are progressing adequately. Some recent changes (particularly as a result of the Schools Act 1992) will ensure that parents receive more information, but not enough has been done to enable parents - probably the majority - who lack confidence (often as a result of their own school experiences), or sufficient knowledge of the system, to get what they want, and what their children are entitled to.

Two consequences arise from this failure: first, it leaves parents who are confident and well-informed in a much stronger position to exert influence, and thus further the interests (and advantage) of their own children; second, it leaves many parents very impressionable, and open to the influence of those they perceive as better informed (whether rightly or not) and thus more powerful. Over recent years, there seems to have been a decline in the level of public, including parents', satisfaction with educational standards in schools. This may be reasonable as comparisons with other countries increasingly show the relative lack of progress in Britain; but there is also a widespread perception that standards have fallen, despite a weight of evidence that, in fact, they have risen (with the exception, perhaps, of reading standards in primary school). Much of this effect on public opinion has been achieved by the publicity given to the views of politicians, and most of the population feels in no position to judge, let alone challenge, the accuracy of those views; most of us have a tendency to accept what we are told by those we think know better than ourselves.

In order to alter this position, there should be more emphasis on empowering all parents through strategies that acknowledge, and seek to redress, the imbalances that exist. Far more could be done in secondary schools to prepare young people for their likely role as parents, and education authorities should have a role alongside health authorities in guiding and encouraging new parents over the development of their babies and young children. There is much evidence to suggest that the differences in development that are already apparent by the time children reach even nursery education (if they are lucky enough to have nursery provision available) are likely to continue, and maybe become greater, throughout their schooling. The contribution that parents make from the birth of their children until they are themselves young adults is now widely recognised - but all too often, parents themselves are not sufficiently aware of it.

There are two separate, but related, aspects of the position of parents: their role in the education of their own children and their more general role in the operation of schools, and hence the system itself. It was the belated recognition of the contribution which parents make to their children's education that led to the pressure for, and subsequent development of, a closer relationship between parents and schools. This has now extended to a significant level of involvement through a variety of home-school links, including such activities as participation in parent-teacher associations (PTAs). It has also given parents an important place in the running of schools, through membership of their governing bodies. Most schools have long recognised and encouraged parents as partners in the process of education; politicians now recognise their importance as consumers (and voters).

The 'parent movement' has been a powerful force for change, supported by many educationists and politicians (both national and local) since the not-so-distant days when many schools displayed signs instructing 'No Parents Beyond This Point'. However, there is still no proper national representative parent body (a point to which we shall return) so, as we saw in Chapter 3, ministers are too freely able to promote policy 'on behalf of' parents whilst dismissing unwelcome views from the various parent organisations that do exist as 'not representing the nation's parents as a whole'. Indeed, there is considerable controversy about the direction of some recent changes, and the extent to which the nation's parents as a whole have sought - or even welcome - much of what has been done in their name.

It was the 'Plowden' Report[7] of the (now abolished) Central Advisory Council for Education[8] in 1967 which most significantly advocated the need for parents to be far more involved than was then (and, to some extent, is still) the case. Drawing on both existing and specially-commissioned research, Plowden established a clear link between parental attitudes and educational attainment, and suggested ways of encouraging parents - especially those with least contact with schools - to become far more actively involved in the education of their children. Recommendations were directed at schools, LEAs and the Government. The report also argued for the redistribution of educational resources to enable schools to compensate children for the effects of social and financial deprivation.

Aspects of the Plowden report have been much maligned by the political 'right' for the part they are alleged to have played in overturning 'traditional' methods of teaching, but most such criticism is ill-founded. Established by a Conservative government in 1963 'to consider primary education in all its aspects, and the transition to secondary education', the membership of the Council represented a broad range of perspectives. Its report, presented to a Labour Secretary of State over three years later, ran to more than 500 pages, with a further volume (of over 600 pages) of research and surveys. It was soundly-based, well-argued, specific in its identification of strategies and realistic in recognising that priorities must be set in a situation where resources were limited. The fact that, a quarter of a century after its publication, some of the progress to which it led is being reversed without any comparable body of evidence to support such changes is illustrative of a change in the approach to policy formation. Ironically perhaps, a number of recent changes - for example, the greater emphasis on parents' right to more information on their children's progress in school and on schools themselves - are amongst recommendations in the report that have taken a long time to be substantially implemented (though Plowden does not seem to have been acknowledged as a source of such policy).

The Plowden Report also recommended that governing bodies should include parents of children attending the school, and that the whole system of school governance should be made clearer and more accessible and comprehensible to parents. Subsequent reports took up this theme, and eventually the Taylor Committee was appointed to review the position and make recommendations.

Up until that time, governing bodies (or managing bodies, as they were in primary schools) were appointed by the LEA with considerable variation in practice. Many schools (especially primaries) had shared governing bodies; some included parents, but most did not. The Taylor Report recommendations included: that each school should have its own governing body (and that the distinction from managing bodies in primary schools should be dropped); that the membership should consist of equal numbers representing the LEA, parents, staff (both teaching and non-teaching) and the local community - with the last group being co-opted by the others; that, except for specifically confidential matters, governors' agendas and minutes should be made available; that parents' organisations should be encouraged (including, where possible, by the provision of facilities) and that governing bodies should satisfy themselves that adequate arrangements existed to inform and involve parents and give them reasonable access to the school and teachers.

It was the 1980 Education Act that introduced a number of these changes, though some of Taylor's proposals - most significantly the one on equal representation on governing bodies - were not accepted. Under the 1980 Act (not fully implemented until September 1985), each school governing body had to include at least two *elected* parent governors (except voluntary-aided and special agreement schools, which had to have at least one elected and one appointed parent governor) and at least one elected teacher governor in schools with fewer than three hundred pupils and at least two in larger schools.

The same Act gave parents the right to express a preference for the school they would like their child(ren) to attend; the right to have that preference complied with except in specified circumstances and the right to appeal to a panel (the decision of which would be binding on the LEA or governing body concerned) if they failed to obtain a place at the school of their choice. It also required the publication by LEAs and schools of certain information - including details of admissions policies and arrangements. More controversially, the Act introduced the Assisted Places Scheme, under which (means tested) financial assistance from the Government was made available to a limited number of pupils to enable them to attend fee-paying, independent ('public') schools - a measure seen as providing financial assistance just as much to the schools as to the pupils concerned.

The Education (No.2) Act 1986 increased the representation of parents and the local community and made changes to the powers and duties of governing bodies, introducing the requirement for an annual report to parents and an annual meeting with parents to discuss the report and any other matters concerning the running of the school. Changes to the composition of governing bodies took place in September 1988 in county schools, and the four-year term of office has given rise to a major turnover of governors in September 1992. The 1986 Act compositions still apply, except in GM schools. We have discussed (in Chapter 2) the major changes arising from the 1988 Act.

In September 1991 - with an election approaching and the Schools Bill about to be published - the Government produced 'The Parent's (*sic*) Charter', the first lines of which are: 'This Charter will help you to become a more effective partner in your child's education. As a parent you have important responsibilities. Good schools work better if they have your active support.' The Charter caused a storm of controversy, mainly because it was felt to be an abuse of the Government's position to use public funds, the Education Department and schools to distribute what was widely perceived as a political document intended to influence the electorate. Many headteachers refused to distribute it.

The Charter described the present position and existing rights of parents *and* those changes arising from the proposed legislation (which there would not have been time to deal with had the election been called earlier). The 1992 Schools Act requires schools to provide parents with a written report on their children's progress at least once a year and specifies the information that must be included. It also requires the annual publication of 'comparable information' (league tables) about all schools - including LEA schools, GM schools, City Technology Colleges and independent schools - in each area. Such information will include exam and National Curriculum test results, 'destinations' (ie. how many pupils go on to university, college and employment) and truancy rates.

The league tables will present 'crude' information. That is, there will be no adjustment of figures to reflect the different circumstances - and intakes - of schools. Critics of this approach argued strongly, but unsuccessfully, that such factors should be taken into account, and the tables weighted accordingly, for two reasons. Firstly, the most advantaged schools, and those serving the most advantaged communities, will tend to be highly placed, thus increasing their attraction to those (generally more advantaged) parents who are in the best position to exercise choice - and adding to the disadvantage of the schools already experiencing it. Secondly, such figures will give no measure of the real performance of schools; the 'value added' by the school to the particular pupils it serves. In other words, two schools may produce similar results from quite different intakes, where one receives pupils with a much higher initial level of performance than the other. Crude information, which simply reports that both have a similar output, will mask the fact that the one which receives pupils at the higher level is plainly not achieving as much progress as the one where pupils began from a lower level - which, therefore, may be a much 'better' school. There is little evidence that parents are sufficiently aware of the different characteristics of the schools in their area to be able to interpret crude data for themselves other than in a similarly crude manner, which does raise doubts about the motivation behind the new requirements.

So, considerable progress has been made in terms of advancing the position of parents within the education system in the last twenty-five years. But is it the progress that parents would have wished? And do all parents wish for the same? And what is the significance of the differences?

The fact that there is no national representative body for parents is a considerable hindrance to the effective expression of parental views. The author argued in 1986 (in an article in the *TES*) for the creation of such a body, based on elected parent governors. The proposal was that each LEA should establish a consultative committee of representative parent governors (with local committees in large authorities) elected by all the parent governors in the relevant area;[9] the chairs of each LEA consultative committee should constitute the membership of a national body, with a regional structure - the chairs of each regional committee forming a national committee which, completely democratically, could genuinely speak for parents as a whole (at least to the same extent as politicians speak for the public).

In this system LEAs would be responsible for establishing their level of the structure, which would strengthen the role of parents locally. The Department for Education would establish, and support, the regional and national tiers, which would greatly strengthen the role of parents in the development and implementation of national policy. The opportunity to significantly influence policy, locally and nationally as well as within individual schools, would make the role of parent governors even more meaningful and rewarding, thus encouraging a greater level of parental interest both in the election of parent governors and in standing for election themselves.

The creation of a genuinely democratic, national parent representative body would greatly enhance the influence that parents could exert. As the greater autonomy of schools leads to the increasing fragmentation of the present system, such a body would also enable parents to keep in touch more effectively with developments in schools elsewhere in the country. It is hard to see what objection a government seriously committed to promoting the position of parents could have to establishing such a structure.

Although such bodies as the National Confederation of Parent Teacher Associations, the Campaign for State Education and the Advisory Centre for Education do an excellent job in promoting the position of parents, they are limited by their nature as voluntary organisations. In the absence of a truly representative voice for parents, anyone, from the author to ministers, can find backing for their own point of view. However, the author can at least confidently claim to have been in contact with far more parents around the country than any politician. The resulting impression, simply on the issue of the position of parents within the school system, is that there is general approval for the provision of more information - but that it should be meaningful information. While most parents would probably agree that the role of parent governors is useful at school level (if of little significance on a broader basis), the majority are not sufficiently enthusiastic even to participate in their election, let alone to put themselves forward as candidates. The expanding work-load and pressure on governors in the face of increasing delegation of responsibility, and simultaneously decreasing budgets, certainly deters many parents (and others) from becoming governors. There is little evidence that the majority of parents want to be involved in the running of schools. Attendance at the obligatory annual meeting between governors and parents is well below ten per cent in a great many schools - unless there is a problem.

I have already referred to the role of parents as consumers, but there are obvious problems over treating education simply as a commodity in the market. If shoppers don't like the selection or quality of goods at a particular store, they can shop elsewhere. However, unless they live near a shopping centre, where there is variety of choice, this may be quite difficult in practice. Their only alternative is to take the matter up with the proprietor in the hope that the situation can be improved. If their views are widely shared the proprietor would be foolish not to respond, but if their demands are not widespread they may be unlucky; the proprietor may even be quite happy if a few awkward customers shop elsewhere. Unusual needs are generally only accommodated in specialist outlets - normally at premium prices.

When seeking school provision for their children, most parents are fairly limited in their choice; many have virtually none. Even where a reasonable choice does exist, once it has been made it is very disruptive to subsequently change it, and most parents would regard moving a child to a different school through dissatisfaction as a last resort. If the widely varying needs of large numbers of children are to be met within an area then schools must be responsive to all their parents. One of the problems that will inevitably accompany the fragmentation of the school system is that minority groups, or those seeking specialist provision, lose the opportunity to influence provision through the collective pressure they are able to exert in an area.

It is not at all apparent that GM schools will be more accountable to parents; indeed, if they are popular, they (as with any over-subscribed school) will increasingly be able to select their pupils rather than parents choosing the schools. By placing control of schools in the hands of a relatively small number of largely appointed governors, the mechanisms through which accountability will function are considerably fewer than in a LEA school where, beyond the governing body, the authority is accountable through its elected members. A substantial increase in the number of schools opting out, and the consequent loss of that level of accountability, would lead to a major diminution in the democratic nature of this vitally important public service.

Even where GM schools are genuinely responsive to their parents, there is no mechanism for accountability to the parents of children who are unable to gain admission to the schools, or who are excluded from them; nor is there accountability to the general community which funds the schools. Where GM schools are not responsive to parents, the next stop in search of a remedy is the Secretary of State. Doubtless many parents would try and enlist the support of their local Member of Parliament, and MPs can certainly expect to see education becoming a very much greater part of their constituency work in areas where the GM sector expands.

The manner in which some governing bodies, and some headteachers, have treated parents in order to get their own way over schools opting out does not suggest that, having got what they wanted, they will subsequently become models of accountability. (The procedure for opting out, and how it is practised - including the role and rights of parents - is covered in Chapter 7.) Local authorities are sometimes accused of ignoring the wishes of parents, and behaving as if they 'know best', but schools - and, indeed, governments - are often just as guilty of exactly those faults; and they are often able to exercise their advantage of power over parents more directly.

The White Paper makes a number of proposals which are relevant to the issues of choice and accountability; these are discussed in Chapter 11.

NOTES

1   *School Governors: A New Role,* Des 1988.
2   Special-agreement schools are very similar to voluntary-aided schools, but LEAs contribute to the cost of the buildings.
3   Where there are two tiers of local government (county and district councils), the lower tier is the minor authority.
4   *A New Partnership for our Schools,* DES 1978.
5   *The Role and Function of Governing Bodies of Grant-Maintained Schools,* DFE, March 1992.
6   *Education,* 5.6.92.
7   *Children and their Primary Schools,* HMSO, 1967.
8   The 1944 Act required ministers to set up the Central Advisory Council for Education; it was scrapped by the 1986 Act, which was drafted when Sir Keith Joseph was Secretary of State.
9   Such a model existed - with local and central committees - extremely successfully in the Inner London Education Authority. It gave parents a very influential voice in the affairs of the Authority; it was also represented on the Education Committee and on sub-committees. The author became more broadly involved in the education service as a direct consequence of his role as a parent governor and chair of his local and the central Parents Consultative Committee.

5
HEADS AND STAFF

A school's staff is its most valuable asset. The finest buildings will not make a good school, and most parents set the highest priority on having good teachers for their children, and recognise the need for teachers to be happy with their working conditions. For obvious reasons, the headteacher is the most critical individual member of the staff. S/he has a crucial role as the overall manager of the school, with responsibility for its day-to-day operation, including line-management of almost all the other people working in the school.

Depending on the size and internal organisation of the school, the head will be assisted by a senior management team, consisting of any deputy-heads and possibly other senior staff (year or department heads). In addition to the teaching staff, some of the following will work in the school: administrative staff, cleaners, school meals staff, mid-day supervisors, schoolkeepers and caretakers, classroom assistants, technicians, librarians and media resource officers. All make their own contribution to the success of a school.

Whether the headteacher is a governor or not (which is their choice, except in a GM school), the governing body is likely to work closely with them, and to depend greatly upon them for advice and guidance. The personality of the head often shapes the 'personality' of the school - and the management ability, and style, of the head has been shown to be a critical factor in the 'effectiveness' of the school. The headteacher normally, of course, also carries considerable influence with parents.

For these reasons, the role of the headteacher is of

fundamental importance in a school which is considering opting out. Also, governors, parents and staff should feel able to approach heads for impartial, professional advice. Since they will presumably wish to retain good relations with members of the school community holding a variety of views on opting out whatever the outcome of the issue, the way in which headteachers conduct themselves is likely to have some effect on their own futures. The headteacher associations advised their members to 'approach the matter with great caution' (Secondary Heads Association) and not to 'adopt too high a profile' (National Association of Headteachers). As we shall see in Chapter 7, this advice has often been ignored.

For the staff of a school, opting out brings many potential changes - but they have no part in the formal procedures except a right to see the same material as parents receive with their ballot papers and the right (as any other member of the public) to object to the proposals when submitted. Parents are usually keen to know the attitude of the staff, especially teachers, to the prospect of their school opting out. It therefore seems a reasonable and wise course of action, even if not one required by the Act, to give staff the same opportunity as parents to express a view on opting out through a secret ballot (so that they do not feel inhibited by the views of colleagues, or senior managers), and to let parents know the outcome before having to vote in their ballot.

Heads have found themselves at the forefront of the many changes affecting schools in recent years. The burden of responsibility, and volume of work, placed upon them has grown considerably; even more so than upon their colleagues, many of whom have also experienced substantial extra demands on their time and energy. The 1986 Act put clear, and specific, responsibilities on heads; the 1988 Act brought the National Curriculum, testing and assessment, LMS and open enrolment. 'League tables' of exam results and other criteria lie just around the corner. Schools have been put into an environment where, as we have seen, they are subject as never before to market forces. For all schools, this brings opportunities and challenges; for some it brings enormous difficulties and very real threats. As the managers of schools, it is heads that are at the sharp end of these pressures. Different individuals react to this situation in different ways; their reaction is often linked to the particular circumstances of their school - which have a major effect on the difficulty of the task they face, often for reasons which are beyond anyone's control.

As we have seen, the issue of opting out arises for a number of reasons: the threat of closure; shortage of money; status; political pressure; and sometimes for no obvious reason. The role of the head in initiating and/or overseeing the process of discussion varies greatly. Sometimes - regardless of the advice of their professional associations - it is the head who raises the issue and makes much of the running; sometimes the head feels obliged to make plain her/his opposition to, or reservations about, the idea. Since the issue has not yet been formally considered at all in the vast majority of schools, it is reasonable to conclude that, although there may be many factors influencing their position (including the advice of their associations), the vast majority of headteachers have not found the 'opportunity' it presents sufficiently attractive to make them want to pursue it.

There is little evidence that the attitude of heads has changed in the aftermath of the 1992 general election - despite the widespread speculation about the apparent inevitability of an avalanche of schools opting out. A telephone survey of heads in the *TES* of 1 May 1992 suggested that heads - especially in those areas where some schools have already opted out - may be more resigned to the increased pressure to follow suit, in order to maintain the competitive position of their school, but that most remain either opposed to such a trend or, at least, unconvinced that it will bring worthwhile benefits. The irony of schools being pressured into considering opting out because neighbouring schools are likely to be doing so is, of course, that those schools are probably doing it for the same reason. (The Lemming Approach to opting out.) One key role for heads (collectively), as 'joint managers' of the school system, is to liaise with each other locally to avoid the situation where events are determined by anxiety, suspicion and even hysteria, rather than by sensible - and educationally-based - consideration of the issues involved. Heads probably have better established networks than anyone else for this purpose, and many are already actively using them.

There is already talk of 'holding lines' and the problems of 'breaking rank', which is symptomatic of the increased pressures of competition to which schools are now subject - often to the strongly-felt regret of heads who fear that present developments will create a two-tier system that will leave many pupils worse off. This applies not only to the issue of opting out amongst schools which have yet to consider it but also, for example, to the issue of selection amongst the schools in the small number of areas where a significant proportion of the secondary sector is already grant-maintained. In most areas, heads are accustomed to working fairly closely together. Unless positive steps are taken to prevent it, the new situation created by the much greater influence of market forces on the relative success of their schools makes relationships with colleagues far more competitive and less co-operative. There is a greater tendency to mutual wariness or even suspicion, which may result in pupils suffering rather than benefiting. Most heads are apparently determined to avoid these dangers; it is the small proportion with a different perspective that gives their colleagues cause for concern - the ones that are likely to break ranks.

One should not generalise about headteachers any more than about other groups of people, but there are certain characteristics that will be recognisable to many amongst the heads they know. Briefly, the significant characteristics that have been commonly observed amongst the heads that have encouraged their schools to consider opting out (for reasons other than an immediate threat to the future of their school arising from reorganisation proposals or budget crises) are as follows:

ambition and/or a competitive nature, now being given the opportunity to flourish. In many cases this is plainly directed towards the benefit of the the pupils in their school; in others it may be directed more towards enhancing their personal position.

a tendency to autocracy, which GM status certainly enhances. Some heads have plainly relished the prospect of no longer being part of a system, whilst gaining additional power within their own 'empire'; others have simply felt (with a confidence that may sometimes be misplaced) that they could manage the school better on their own.

a desire for change, but not too much. A number of the heads that have been active in pursuing GM status for their schools have been in post for a considerable period and, presumably, have found the professional stimulus of opting out more attractive than that of moving on to another school.

a lack of sympathy with the political/educational objectives of the LEA of which the school is part.

The extent to which such characteristics are apparent to, and welcomed by, the rest of the school community is a major factor in determining the outcome of any discussion of opting out. The conduct of the procedures for such discussion are considered in Chapter 7.

There are a number of ways in which a school opting out may affect the staff, collectively or individually. As the Department for Education Circular 10/88 on opting out explained:

Staff who work solely at a school which becomes grant-maintained will transfer to the employment of the governing body ... Staff cannot refuse to transfer .. other than by resigning or being assigned elsewhere by the LEA ... All the rights, powers, duties and liabilities of the former employer (the LEA) ... will transfer to the governing body ... The (GM) schools will have to comply with the same regulations as LEA schools in relation to the employment of teachers and other staff. Pay and conditions for new non-teaching staff will be agreed between those staff and the governing body. As an employer, the governing body will become responsible under health and safety legislation for the health and safety of its staff as well as of the pupils and others present at the school.

Thus, if staff do not wish to go on working in a school which has opted out, their only option is to resign. However, this is not likely to be attractive, or even realistic, for most people, even if they feel strongly about the issue. There are a number of reasons why members of staff may not wish the school in which they work to opt out. They may be opposed, in principle, to the concept of opting out (they did not, after all, choose to work in a GM school and have virtually no part in the choice of whether the school opts out or not).

The fact that the governing body may lack the skills and experience staff would expect of an employer may cause great concern, especially as disciplinary and grievance procedures will be restricted to the governing body. Staff may be anxious about the potential problems arising from the destruction of the delicate balance of relationships that keeps most schools on an even keel, and the increased autonomy - or at least influence - of the head.

They may fear that trade union recognition would be limited, as it has been in some GM schools, and that they could find themselves without adequate representation to negotiate with the governing body over pay and conditions. According to Peter Smith, General Secretary of AMMA, only one quarter of GM schools have officially recognised the union for negotiating purposes.[1]

They may value the services of the LEA, and not wish to find themselves denied or restricted in their access to them. Teachers in particular may be concerned about the reduced contact they would probably have with colleagues from other local schools during in-service training and other LEA-based activities. Such contact is very important to many teachers, who spend a great deal of time 'isolated' in their class-rooms.

There is also considerable suspicion about the longer-term effects of opting out on the terms and conditions of employment of staff. It is already the case that governing bodies of GM schools may negotiate their own terms when filling non-teaching posts. Since April 1992, it has also been possible for individual GM schools, or for LEAs (but *not* individual LEA schools), to seek exemption from the national School Teachers' Pay and Conditions Document. In a guidance note for governors of GM schools, the Department for Education points out that, following exemption, they 'can draw up contracts for their teachers which make different provision as to duties, working time or pay arrangements from those contained in the Document'.[2]

When a school opts out, staff working solely in the school have their contracts of employment (and thus any *contractual* benefits) transferred from the LEA to the governing body. (Most staff in voluntary aided schools are already employed by their governing bodies, so this would be less of a change for them; however, the governing body of a GM school does not enjoy the support and services of the LEA - including those of the personnel department - that are available as of right to LEA-maintained schools, including those which are voluntary aided.) Staff who work part-time in a school which opts out and also work in other schools may be transferred as well, in which case their whole contract would switch to the GM school, which would 'hire back' the person's part-time services to the other school(s) involved. Staff employed in the school meals service are considered to work solely *at* the school only if the meals they produce are solely *for* the school.

Some staff will be employed in areas of work that are subject to Compulsory Competitive Tendering (CCT), under the Local Government Act 1988. These areas (in schools) are catering, cleaning and grounds maintenance, the arrangements for which are now subject to 'contracts' that need careful consideration where opting out is concerned. Most such contracts are with councils' own ('in-house') Direct Service Organisations (DSOs) - in which case the staff are still employed by the local authority. If they work solely at one school, their employment will therefore be subject to transfer to the governing body if the school opts out. If, as with most grounds maintenance and some cleaning, the staff work in more than one school the situation is more complex. If the contract is 'in-house' (ie. with the council's DSO) then opting out schools generally appear to be able to leave it if they wish. If it is a contract with a private organisation, they are bound by its terms until it comes up for renewal. All schools (GM and LMS) will be able to re-negotiate such arrangements (whether with DSOs or private contractors) when they are due for renewal. This means that the only major differences between GM and LMS schools will be over the timing of any change, and who actually employs the staff.

There have been some disturbing examples of non-teaching staff being treated very badly over opting out. Some governing bodies wishing to leave CCT arrangements have sought to avoid the transfer of staff, particularly catering staff, to their employment in order to be able to purchase school meals from a private contractor. Industrial Tribunal proceedings, and possibly further legal action, are being pursued at the time of writing.

Whilst such cases are extreme (but likely to become more numerous if opting out becomes widespread), there are other issues of employment rights and conditions of service which could affect any member of staff. Some employment benefits are statutory (ie. have to be offered as a result of legislation); others are discretionary (ie. are offered at the discretion of the employer, usually as a result of negotiation between trade unions and employers). Some of the discretionary rights are national (arising from collective agreements between the unions and the local authority organisations); others are local (arising from agreements between single employers and their staff's union representatives). Local discretionary benefits may or may not be incorporated into the contract of employment (and will transfer automatically only if they are); national ones are more likely to be, and statutory benefits are bound to be.

Discretionary benefits may offer improvements on statutory terms, or they may cover areas for which there is no statutory provision. In some cases, such rights are only acquired after a period of continuous employment with an employer (eg. the right to take a case for unfair dismissal to an Industrial Tribunal); in others, entitlement improves with longer service (eg. sick leave, maternity leave and holidays). When moving from one employer to another, discretionary benefits are therefore usually lost, and are acquired again only after a period with the new employer. Although continuous local government service is 'transferable' for some purposes, service in LEAs and GM schools is only regarded as continuous for the purposes of statutory benefits (eg. pension rights). Whilst existing contractual terms and conditions are protected when a school opts out and contracts transfer to the new governing body, problems over discretionary benefits may arise when staff then seek work elsewhere. Transferring between two LEA schools in the same authority does not affect discretionary benefits, as there is no change of employer; however, if staff transfer between a LEA school and a GM school they may lose benefits.

The present situation opens the door not only for staff in different GM schools being treated differently - and differently from staff in LEA schools - but also for similar staff within the same GM school to be treated differently, depending on whether their contracts were transferred on opting out or they were appointed after that, on whatever terms the governing body felt appropriate (depending, presumably, on the employment market for the particular post). Of course, this may work to the advantage of staff in GM schools, who may find that the school is willing, and able, to pay higher rates - or even employ more staff. This possibility is certainly a feature of many of the attempts to persuade parents (and staff) of the advantages of opting out. Just how sustainable such claims will prove in a situation where large numbers of schools opted out, and financial provision was reduced, remains to be seen. A school that has entered into such commitments during favourable times will face added problems should circumstances worsen, which would give added weight to some of the anxieties described here.

The issue of GM schools paying teachers - particularly headteachers - more money is one that may have a bearing not only on the attitude of heads and staff towards opting out, but on the procedures themselves. It is an accepted principle that individuals should not have a role in making decisions over the expenditure of public funds if they have a pecuniary interest in the outcome of the decision. It was established in the Court of Appeal that teacher governors (including headteachers) are not entitled to vote on a proposal that a school should become a City Technology College, in which their salaries may be higher.[3]

Legal action on the same grounds, but involving a school becoming grant-maintained, was taken over the pecuniary interest of four governors of Small Heath School, Birmingham (the head, two teachers and a parent governor who was a non-teaching employee at the school). Although the action was successful in the Divisional Court, the judgement was reversed in the Appeal Court - where, coincidentally, the same judge (Lord Justice Glidewell) as in the CTC case delivered the leading judgement. The Appeal Court took the view that there were materially significant differences between CTCs and GM schools; one of these differences being that 'teachers at a CTC would probably work longer hours ... and thus earn more.'

However, as we have seen, exactly the same may now happen in GM schools. Moreover, there is widespread evidence of some teachers - particularly heads - being paid more when schools opt out. The *TES* of 8 February 1991 led on its front page with the news that 'One of the first schools to opt out of local authority control now has the highest paid head in the state sector'. According to the *TES*, the governors of the London Oratory School raised the salary of the head, John McIntosh, from just over £30,000 to 'around £50,000' within eighteen months. (Incidentally, the *Daily Telegraph* of 30 December 1989 reported that 'Mr McIntosh, who is a member of the Centre for Policy Studies [one of the organisations referred to in Chapter 3], played an influential role in formulating the concept of opting out which ministers were later persuaded to take up.') It may be that, in the new circumstances of GM schools, the issue of pecuniary interest should be looked at again. As Cecil Knight, the head of Small Heath School, has written in describing his experience of the legal proceedings referred to above, 'We stood to gain nothing but the satisfaction of doing a better job. *Had the present pay and conditions document been in force, it would have been a different matter. I would now be free to negotiate a salary commensurate with my greater responsibilities.*'[4] (Author's emphasis)

Another source of concern is that of staff discipline, dismissal and appeals. Every GM school governing body must establish a staff committee and an appeal committee, and no governor may be on both. The staff committee establishes disciplinary rules and procedures; either it or the head may suspend a member of staff, but only the committee may end a suspension. The staff committee also has the power to dismiss staff. Should this occur, the member of staff may appeal against dismissal to the appeal committee. However, many staff feel it is very unsatisfactory that the only appeal against dismissal by one group of governors is to another group of governors. The only other form of redress is to an Industrial Tribunal (a right acquired only after two years continuous service) or the Courts. In an LEA school, the situation is similar, but there is more likelihood of the governors following the authority's personnel practice, and of the advice of its personnel department being taken. As the employer, the Chief Education Officer is entitled to be present (or represented) at proceedings. These are significant safeguards.

Redundancy in GM schools also presents potential problems. In a situation of market forces, mobile pupil populations and surplus capacity some schools are likely to contract - which will lead to the shedding of staff. Whatever advantage it is believed opting out brings in terms of competition for pupils, GM schools are unlikely to be immune from this problem - especially in an area where there are several such schools. The Department for Education acknowledges this by making a grant available to cover the costs of such restructuring as is agreed during the first year after opting out. Severance costs arising after that will have to be borne by the school; this is likely to exert a greater influence on who is to go than the demands of the curriculum. It is also likely to inhibit opportunities for early retirement. Severence costs from LEA schools are borne by the authority, which is also likely to operate a co-operative redeployment scheme amongst its schools.

In-service training opportunities for staff are likely to be different in a GM school, which may buy into the LEA provision or may choose to go elsewhere, or may find that the LEA gives priority to the staff of its own schools. In either case, there will be a reduction in the contact with local colleagues which many staff value highly.

If staff are really valued, their concerns must be listened to - and should form a key part of the decision-making process. It may be possible to offer reassurance on a number of points, for example, trade-union recognition and time-off for trade-union duties (including health and safety work); time off for public duties (as a councillor or magistrate, for example); the continuance of equal opportunity policies; and continuing guarantees for pay and conditions. The position of non-teaching staff should be respected just as much as that of teachers. Unfortunately, such reassurances cannot be offered as guarantees, and the behaviour of a small number of the governing bodies of existing GM schools has not been helpful.

NOTES

1   *TES*, 19.6.92.
2   *The Role and Function of Governing Bodies of Grant-Maintained Schools*, DES, 1992.
3   Law Report, *Independent*, 17.4.1989.
4   Brent Davies and Lesley Anderson, *Opting for Self-Management*, Routledge, London 1992.

6
FINANCIAL ARRANGEMENTS FOR GM SCHOOLS

A vital point to grasp when considering opting out is that it is not possible to predict accurately how much a school would get in its budget if it was grant-maintained. This is because all the factors which determine the levels of the grants the school might receive are decided outside the school, many on an annual basis. These have already been changed several times, as we shall see later and the White Paper makes two things quite clear: firstly, the levels of grant to GM schools are to be reduced in future, and will depend on the government's annual Public Spending Survey; secondly, a new system of funding for GM schools is to be phased in from April 1994 that will give the government direct control over the expenditure on GM schools. (These points are discussed in Chapter 10; this chapter deals with the present system.) This means that there is little value in the kind of financial comparisons that are often presented to parents, which usually seek to show a major financial gain from opting out.

It is a strange thing, but many advocates of opting out say that money is not the important thing: ministers have said that GM schools are not treated more favourably than others (except, temporarily, in respect of capital); the Department for Education says that 'In some respects schools do not change because they have become grant-maintained. They are funded at the same level as they would have been had they remained with their LEA'.[1] Yet, in all the author's experience of meetings and the literature sent to parents, it is nearly always money that dominates and, specifically, how much more the school would get if it opted out. So, it clearly *is* important - if only because it seems to be the view that parents need convincing that the school will gain financially before they will vote for it to opt out. What is less clear is whether or not GM schools do get more money, and - if they do - how much more, and for how much longer.

The Secretary of State is required by the 1988 Act (Section 79) to pay an annual maintenance grant to GM schools 'such as may be determined (and from time to time revised) in accordance with regulations made by the Secretary of State'. Grant regulations 'may also provide' for the payment of special purpose grants and capital grants. Notice that the only payment the Secretary of State is *required* to make is the annual maintenance grant, the amount of which depends on regulations made by himself, under which he *may* also pay special purpose grant and capital grant. Annual maintenance grant is recovered directly from the LEA which formerly maintained the GM school; other grants are recovered indirectly through more general adjustments to local authorities' finances.

Also, the Secretary of State has powers to impose, waive, remove or vary requirements in respect of grant payments, with which governing bodies are obliged to comply; requirements may be imposed before, at or after the time when payments are made. If governing bodies fail to comply with requirements, they may have to repay, in whole or in part, grant payments they have received.

From all this, it is quite clear that the Secretary of State is able to vary the position easily and, indeed, new regulations are issued for each financial year, although they do not necessarily alter every grant. We shall now look at what happens when a school opts out, and at how it is then funded.

On the incorporation date, the property, rights and liabilities (excluding debt charges) of the former maintaining authority and those (if any) of the former governing body, are transferred to and vested in the governing body of the GM school. The school is then funded directly by the Department for Education through the grants outlined above.

Once a GM application has been approved, the (prospective) governing body may apply, during a period within twelve months of the incorporation date, for a 'transitional grant' to cover expenditure incurred as a result of the change in status of the school. This will include such costs as setting up the necessary accountancy and administrative systems to replace functions previously undertaken for the school by the LEA; a large proportion of approved expenditure is for the hardware and software for such systems.

The *maximum* level of transitional grant for schools with 200 or more pupils is £30,000 plus £30 per pupil (up to a ceiling of £60,000) or, for schools with fewer than 200 pupils, £20,000 plus £30 per pupil. (A pupil who takes the roll of a school from 199 to 200 is thus worth £10,030.) It is a 'one off' grant paid only for approved expenditure on costs arising from the change to GM status. It is therefore misleading to present it to parents (as is frequently done) as a benefit of opting out.

The school's day-to-day running costs are met by the annual maintenance grant (AMG), which has three elements: the LMS formula funding (Budget Share) that the school would have received had it remained in the LEA; an add-on sum in place of the services that the LEA provides centrally to its schools; and a sum in respect of school meals, contingencies and (where appropriate) nursery education.

The first of these is very straightforward. It is only necessary to point out that it is by far the largest of the three elements, and that any changes that affect the formula which the LEA makes to its LMS scheme or to its schools budget will affect GM schools as much as those still within the LEA.

The second element, the central expenditure add-on to replace services previously provided by the LEA, is more complex and - since it is the main difference between being a GM school and a LMS school - it is important to be clear about it.

Before April 1991, 'central expenditure' was calculated on the basis of detailed information submitted by LEAs about their central costs and reflected the actual level of such expenditure by that particular authority. In 1991, this was changed, and all GM schools received a flat-rate add-on of sixteen per cent of the formula funding, regardless of the actual figure in their LEA - the only exception being for schools operating as GM prior to 1 April 1991. (These received sixteen per cent or, where it was higher, the cash amount for full-year central AMG in 1990/91.)

The figure of sixteen per cent was the average of the 'central expenditure' element in the fifty GM schools that existed at that time. These were all secondary schools and were located in only 33 of the 117 LEAs in England and Wales. Thus the percentage could hardly be described as a national average figure for LEAs' central costs. Indeed, the change was greeted with vigorous protests from education authorities - especially those which had already reduced their central costs below this level by delegating more to schools through the LMS formula. It was claimed that the figure was above the true national average for centrally provided services so, in those authorities which had delegated most, it provided schools with an extra financial incentive to opt out. It also meant that any schools which did opt out of those authorities would therefore cost the LEA (through recovery of the AMG) more than it had previously been spending on them, since they would then have both a higher level of formula funding, through greater delegation, and a higher add-on than appropriate. To add insult to injury, since the latter is a percentage of the former, this produced a double gain to the schools, and a double loss to the authorities - which were thus obliged to channel more funding into the GM schools than into their ordinary LEA schools. It also follows that, in an authority where the level of centrally-provided services was above sixteen per cent, this change was a disincentive to opting out, as the 'central expenditure' add-on would be worth less than the services it was intended to replace.

Ironically, one effect of this change was to stop a number of authorities which had been planning to increase levels of delegation to schools from doing so. Thus one aspect of the Government's school policy directly inhibited another: greater devolution intended to benefit schools in general has been slowed as a result of government policy towards GM schools.

For 1992/93, the standard add-on has been reduced to fifteen per cent, to reflect the increased rate of delegation under LMS that took place in the intervening year. It is clearly likely to fall further over the next couple of years, as the rate of delegation increases further - and the smaller this element is, the smaller is the financial difference for a school between being in or out of the LEA (especially since most of the remaining centrally-provided services need to be obtained from somewhere and LEAs are developing their LMS schemes to give increasing flexibility to schools over both the level and source of such services).

A further change for 1992/93 is the introduction of a non-standard add-on to be used (if requested either by a GM school or the LEA) in an authority in which fifteen per cent or more of either the primary or secondary schools (rounded up to a whole number) have opted out. The add-on will then be calculated once more on the basis of actual figures for that authority - so there will no longer be an issue of the standard add-on being greater than appropriate in many LEAs. No school looking at opting out can assume that, if it does, it won't be joined by enough others to pass this threshold, thus putting the central AMG add-on onto this basis; it has already been triggered in a small number of LEAs. It remains to be seen how far, or how fast, the GM sector expands - but this change, and the way in which LMS develops over the next couple of years, could eliminate much of the financial benefit claimed for opting out.

The third element of annual maintenance grant, for meals, contingencies and nursery education, is also straightforward. The meals component is calculated to take account of the number of pupils at the school who are entitled to free meals and the level of subsidy (if any) on meals for the number of other pupils taking them. (Sadly, an increasing number of LEAs are abandoning their meals service as part of the cuts they are being obliged to make. They then provide only packed-lunches for pupils entitled to a free school meal - which, incidentally, is only those whose parents are in receipt of Income Support or Family Credit). LEAs usually have a contingency fund which covers, amongst other things, a specific rise in pupil numbers. GM schools may have their grants adjusted if they inform the Department for Education that they have reached a trigger point that applies under the LMS scheme in their LEA. Where a GM school provides education for under fives, the Secretary of State will determine an amount that he believes is fair and reasonable having regard to provision in comparable maintained schools under the LMS scheme of the LEA. This third element of the grant thus makes no real difference to the level of funding between GM schools and LEA schools.

Annual Maintenance Grant is normally paid in monthly instalments, just before salaries are due to be paid. Governors are under a duty to ensure that it is used solely for the purposes of the school as defined in the Act, in regulations and in the school's Articles of Government.

GM schools may also apply for special purpose grants (SPG) to cover expenditure on a number of items: those for which education support grant is payable to LEAs; the training of any teacher or other member of staff; those which it appears to the Secretary of State cannot reasonably be met from AMG, including any structural survey required by the Secretary of State, the dismissal (including redundancy) or premature retirement of a member of staff, liability for VAT, insurance of the school premises, the meeting of any urgent need occasioned by circumstances outside the control of the governing body; and those for which grant is payable for the education of Travellers and Displaced Persons.

The current (1992/93) level of grant for staff training and curriculum development for GM schools (SPG Development) is £42.50 per pupil (compared with an average of about £28 per pupil received by LEAs in government training grant).

Grant for redundancy/early retirement costs (SPG Restructuring) will only be paid in respect of staff changes approved during the first twelve months following incorporation. Thereafter, they must be met from the school's budget.

On opting out, schools lose their entitlement to exemption from VAT. The grant to cover this new cost (SPG VAT) is set at two and a half per cent of the AMG. However, GM schools automatically acquire charitable status, as a result of which they get relief from rates, which are paid by county schools. (This is only a change in respect of ex-county schools, as ex-voluntary schools would have had charitable status previously - a factor built into LMS schemes.) In the case of ex-county schools, the sum received in rate relief is deducted from the grant for VAT. When calculating any change arising from GM status, it is best to regard these elements as financially neutral.

Grant for the insurance of the school premises is for

only half of the cost, up to a maximum of £6,000 (for 1992/93). The cost of insurance will vary with the size and nature of the site, but for large schools this could be a considerable extra expense.

Special purpose grants may be spent only on the specific purposes for which they are given to a school.

The third source of income for GM schools is grants for capital expenditure, mainly building works or major equipment purchases. Capital grant comes in two forms: formula allocation, which is currently available to all GM schools annually, and major project grants, which are subject to competitive bids within the sector and payable, if awarded, at 100 per cent of the project cost.

The formula allocation is for minor projects of a capital nature (eg. modifications to buildings); it cannot be spent on routine repairs and maintenance, nor carried over into the following year. It is decided annually whether or not there will be a formula allocation, and, if there is, the level at which it will be set. In 1991/92 it was £19,000 per school plus £9 per pupil (50 per cent higher than in 1990/91). However, as more schools - especially a number of small primary schools - have opted out, the level has been altered for 1992/93, to £10,000 per school plus £20 per pupil. This considerably reduces the amount payable to small schools, whilst marginally benefiting large ones (the break-even point being at around 800 pupils). The change reportedly reflected the growing anxiety of ministers over the potentially soaring cost of opting out (to which we shall return).

Grant for named projects is payable at 100 per cent of the cost. This is seen by many voluntary schools as a great attraction, as they currently receive capital funding at only 85 per cent of the cost (the remaining 15 per cent falling to the foundation which owns the school to raise). On the other hand, voluntary schools which opt out lose their current entitlement to 85 per cent grant for repairs; this loss may turn out in the future to be greater than the gain - which will only be made on successful bids for capital projects. Also, the White Paper proposes to enable LEAs to contribute to the capital costs of voluntary schools.

A sum is set aside annually as the Department for Education's budget for capital grant to the GM sector. After deducting the amounts required for formula allocation, committed expenditure and a sum for possible future allocation to schools in the process of opting out, the remainder (still the major part) is the total for which all existing GM schools may bid.

The Secretary of State 'will consider all such bids on their relative merits, taking account of the resources available nationally and the criteria being applied to the distribution of capital allocations for maintained schools' (DES circular 21/89). In practice, GM schools have submitted bids way in excess of the resources available; only about fifteen per cent of the total cost of bids was allocated for 1992/93. Some schools, for which the possibility of capital grant was the main incentive for opting out, have been very disappointed; others have fared rather well, as we shall see shortly. Bids for named projects must be over £6,000 in cost; smaller items are covered by the formula allocation.

GM schools have to make their own arrangements directly with the appropriate department for other government grants that would otherwise be administered by the LEA, particularly TVEI (Technical & Vocational Education Initiative, paid by the Department of Employment) and Section 11 (which is paid by the Home Office for meeting the particular needs - especially language, in schools - of pupils of New Commonwealth origin).

Much has been said about whether or not schools are better funded if they opt out and, as we have already seen, the belief that they are is certainly a major factor -

usually the major factor - in persuading parents to vote for opting out. We shall look now at whether this belief is well founded, first as things are at present, and then as they may be in the future.

Of course, one of the factors built into the procedures for opting out is that the initial decision rests solely with the parents of children already at the school. To a large extent then, the implications for the future (financial and otherwise) tend to be for somebody else to worry about, and the prospect of a short-term advantage from which their own children may benefit is naturally hard to resist. This has often been a feature of discussions of the issue, and the leaders of both major churches - responsible for a great many schools, and possibly better practised at resisting temptation - have expressed views on the subject of opting out.

Bishop David Konstant, education chair of the Catholic Bishops Conference, said: 'Opting out will seriously damage the relationship between schools and the local community. I think also that the principle of opting out encourages selfish elitism and it calls into question the relationship between one school and others in its neighbourhood.'[2] The Archbishop of Canterbury, Dr Carey, linked opting out with the shortage of funds for church schools, saying: 'It is disturbing when, as in some cases, it seems a school is pushed in the direction of opting out simply because this is the means of getting cash from the Department of Education for new buildings'.[3] In the same week, Cardinal Basil Hume expressed the view that 'It is extraordinary to see the way in which grant-maintained schools are quite openly being more generously funded than their counterparts in the maintained sector'.[4]

The original (declared) policy of the Government was that GM schools would be funded on the same basis as LEA schools:

The general principle governing the funding of grant-maintained schools is that the acquisition by a school of grant-maintained status should not change the financial position of either the school or of local community charge payers in the LEA which previously maintained the school. The maintenance grant from the Department [for Education] will be calculated so as to reflect as far as possible the level at which the school would have been funded had it continued to be funded by the LEA, including provision for services provided centrally.[5]

We have already referred to a Department of Education booklet which still claimed in 1991 that GM schools 'are funded at the same level as they would have been had they remained with their LEA'. But in fact, the change to the national standard add-on for central services for 1991/92, which broke the direct link with the funding of schools remaining in the same LEA, had already been announced - so this claim could no longer be made honestly by the time it was published. (As we saw above, whether this change was an incentive or disincentive for a school to opt out would depend on the value of centrally-provided services in its particular LEA.)

In October 1990, at the Conservative Party Conference, John McGregor - then the Secretary of State - announced increases in several of the grants to GM schools (as well as the removal of the lower size limit - previously 300 pupils - on primary schools which were eligible). In an obvious move (covered in more detail in Chapter 3) to increase the number of schools opting out, the maximum level of transitional grant was doubled and the levels of SPG (Development) and the formula allocation of capital were increased by fifty per cent.

From then on, there was no doubt that GM schools were being favourably treated. The main inducement, however, lies in the allocation of capital grant for named projects, on which expenditure has been at a much higher rate compared with capital spending in the LEA sector. (Incidentally, the approval given to LEAs for capital spending is to allow them to borrow the necessary funds; the approval given to GM schools is for straightforward grant.) It is also awarded against differing criteria: LEAs' best (and almost only) chance of capital expenditure is on projects to ensure provision of sufficient school places, or projects linked to the removal of surplus places; for GM schools, however, priority is given to projects (such as new laboratories) linked to the national Curriculum or to health and safety. A criterion for 1993/94 (for GM and LEA schools) will be 'popularity' in relation to bids for school expansion (described in Chapter 2). From 1992/93 there is also a separate capital programme for the Technology Schools Initiative, under which both GM and LEA schools can seek funds for technological development; here, too, GM schools received a disproportionate share of the first allocation.

The levels of allocation of capital grant for each relevant financial year have dramatically favoured GM schools. There are a number of ways in which the figures can be compared (spending per school or spending per pupil - in either case, compared locally or nationally), giving a factor of advantage of between double and four times for the level of spending on GM schools.

Ministers at first put this down to the fact that the schools which had opted out had been neglected by their LEAs. (Since many of the early ones were schools which had opted out to avoid closure plans, it is to be expected that they had not had a great deal spent on them shortly before their planned closure.) They then shifted their ground, becoming more frank:

> When schools become grant-maintained we want to ensure that they are set up on a sound basis, This has led on average, to higher capital allocations for the GM sector in 1991/92 than for LEA-maintained schools. (Tim Eggar, Minister for Education, DES Press Release, 23.1.91)

John Major was even more blunt. In a letter to Doug

MacAvoy, General Secretary of the NUT, he wrote:

> We have made no secret of the fact that grant-maintained schools get preferential treatment in allocating grants to capital expenditure. We look favourably at GM schools in order to encourage the growth of that sector and I am delighted to see numbers are continuing to grow rapidly.[6]

The success with which schools have bid for capital grant has been very mixed. Two examples illustrate this clearly:

Pate's Grammar School, Gloucestershire, was a voluntary-aided school which opted out because it was (literally) falling down: the foundation which owns the school, having (as a VA school) contributed to a new building in the 1960s simply could not afford the required 15 per cent share of the cost of replacing it, which became necessary due to the deterioration of its concrete structure. Their bid for a new school building has resulted in capital grant of £3.5 million so far, with more to come.

By contrast, St Francis Xavier's College, Liverpool, another VA school, has submitted bids totalling almost £14 million over the three years since it opted out; it has been awarded just £232,000 (Apparently undeterred, the head, Brother Francis, has contributed a chapter called 'Managing Capital Development' to a book on GM schools.)[7]

Overall, however, there can be no doubt that, up until now, GM schools *have* been favourably treated in a number of respects - and much is made in promotional material for opting out of how much better off they are, and what they have spent the extra money on.

Equally, there can be no doubt that their good fortune is at the expense of other schools - though this is something that (perhaps not surprisingly) those involved with GM schools are reluctant to admit, even to themselves it appears. However, the logic is irrefutable. The amount spent on schools is limited; decisions on spending are taken at both national and local level, so there is variation across the country, but in either case the school service has to compete with others for its share of total resources. If, within the overall allocation made to schools, changes are made that shift funds towards some, then it *must* be at the expense of others.

Ministers, and those in GM schools, have sought to present a different picture, but it does not bear close scrutiny: they say not only that GM schools are getting only *their share* of resources, but that others are not affected, so let us examine the situation.

As we have seen, GM schools are funded by grant from two original sources, although they receive it all via the Department for Education: maintenance grant is recovered from the relevant LEA, so there is a shift of local resources from the LEA to the GM sector within each authority. The costs of all other grants are borne by the Department for Education, so they give rise to a shift of national resources from the whole LEA sector to the whole GM sector. In the latter case, it is perfectly obvious that the higher levels of funding of GM schools through capital and special purpose grant are at the expense of other schools: the DFE has only a set amount to distribute to all schools; in order to give more to some, it must give less to others.

The issue around maintenance grant is not quite so straightforward, but - since this is by far the largest part of spending on GM schools and has a local (and therefore more direct and obvious) effect, as it is recovered from the LEA - it is important that it is understood.

The element of the maintenance grant that is at issue is the central expenditure add-on for services formerly provided directly by the LEA; the formula funded element is at the same level in both GM and LEA schools. We have already seen that, on opting out, schools get a standard add-on which may or may not reflect the level of centrally-provided services in their own LEA. If it is greater than the actual figure, there can be no doubt that the remaining schools lose out; let us therefore assume an example in which the add-on accurately reflects the level of the LEA's centrally provided services.

That sum, for each school which opts out, is recovered by the Department for Education from the LEA, which then has less money for the provision of services to its remaining schools. It is true, of course, that it has fewer schools to service, so it can make some savings. However, it is virtually impossible to make pro rata reductions, so the LEA has two choices - both problematic. It can top up the non-delegated (central services) part of its schools budget to sustain the same level of service, but only to a limited extent for it must remain within the requirement to delegate at least eighty-five per cent of its potential schools budget (and the remaining schools will anyway still be seeking greater delegation). This option would also require equivalent cuts elsewhere in the education budget, or an increase in the education budget at the expense of another service budget, or an increase in the council's overall budget - and hence in the local tax - or a combination of these measures. The only, and more likely, alternative is to reduce the level of service to its remaining schools. It can also sell its central services - at a commercial rate - to GM schools (to a limited extent, both in its own area and beyond), but if GM schools were to spend all their add-on buying back those services from the LEA, there would be little point in opting out.

The problem is largely economy of scale. If a cake is cut into slices, some gets wasted as crumbs; the more slices into which it is cut, the less of the cake ends up on individual plates. If some guests are guaranteed a slice of a particular size, the consequences for their less-favoured companions are obvious.

The apparently contradictory statements that 'GM schools get only their share of resources' and 'the additional funding received by GM schools is at the expense of others' may thus both be true. However, it is an inescapable fact that by opting out and removing their share of resources from the communal total, GM schools are reducing the resources available to others.

There is another factor - of particular relevance to primary schools - which is very important. The standard add-on for central services is a percentage of the formula-funded budget. Since formula funding is age-weighted (for perfectly good reasons), the add-on becomes age-weighted (but in this case, for no good reason at all; in fact, it is obviously ridiculous - and severely penalises primary schools).

The age-weighting factor varies from one LEA scheme to another but, on average, the Age Weighted Pupil Unit for secondary pupils is around fifty per cent greater that for primary pupils. Thus, the add-on is equally weighted towards secondary pupils. So, a secondary school with one thousand pupils which opts out will get an add-on that is fifty per cent greater than the combined add-ons of five primary schools each with two hundred pupils were they to opt out of the same LEA. Yet, it must be almost universally true that primary schools make more use than secondary schools of the central services for which the add-on exists.

When a school opts out, the loss to the LEA will be particularly felt by the remaining schools which make most use of the authority's centrally-provided services - primary schools. Because of the age-weighting factor being applied to the add-on, the effect is much greater as a result of secondary schools opting out. And primary schools cannot even look to opting out themselves to make good the loss they suffer as a result of secondary schools leaving the authority, because the add-on they would receive is age-weighted at the lower level.

This may be a small factor in explaining why opting out is much more prevalent amongst secondary schools, but it is a significant factor in explaining why parents with children in both secondary and primary schools are often strongly opposed to the former opting out. This situation is absurd and damaging, and should not be allowed to continue.

The new non-standard add-on, applied only once fifteen per cent of either the secondary or (conceivably) primary schools opt out of a LEA, will change this. Calculation of the non-standard add-on reverts to a basis which does not introduce an age-weighting factor. This, of course, is a tacit admission of the fault in the standard add-on system - which ministers and the Department have hitherto unconvincingly attempted to defend. It is now time to drop any pretence that it is defensible. There is no excuse (and never was) for having a national flat rate add-on anyway: the method of calculation for the new non-standard version is so simple, and the information required (specific to each LEA) so basic, that it would be quite straightforward to use it for all schools which opt out. The fact that ministers insisted on, or allowed, the introduction of an unjust, irrational and unnecessary (but administratively more convenient) standard method is exactly the kind of behaviour they are fond of attributing to LEAs.

There is one remaining problem, even once the non-standard model is applied, and that is the built-in protection for the budgets of existing GM schools. The add-on for such schools cannot (under present regulations) be lower than the cash value of the add-on for the previous year. There is no obvious, similar protection offered to the budgets of any other kind of school. It means that, even where a school has demonstrably enjoyed the benefit of a higher level of funding for central services than is justified, it will continue to do so for some time - at the expense of other schools in the area.

We have already seen that the additional benefits enjoyed by GM schools fall as additional costs to either LEAs or the Department for Education; the implications of a major extension of opting out are obviously considerable - not least for GM schools themselves; both those that already exist and those that may opt out in the future. Any school looking at opting out from now on must weigh these up very carefully - especially in view of the new funding arrangements proposed in the White Paper (discussed in Chapter 11).

It is quite clear that during the period between the introduction of the 1988 Act and the 1992 general election, the Government was prepared to spend considerable sums of (taxpayers') money to promote its policy of opting out (as the Prime Minister's letter to Doug MacAvoy makes clear). It is now equally clear that existing levels of grant cannot be sustained for more than a *very* short time - especially if, as we are told, there is to be considerable pressure from the Treasury to reduce public expenditure in the coming few years.

The most detailed consideration of this matter so far published is a report by Tony Bush and Marianne Coleman (respectively Professor of, and Research Associate in, Educational Management at the University of Leicester).[8] The report examined all aspects of the funding of GM schools and projected the costs of an extension of opting out amongst secondary schools to totals of two and four thousand (both figures having been claimed as numbers which might opt out, the latter being the whole of the secondary sector).

Bush and Coleman's analysis divides the extra funds received by the GM sector into those which represent a transfer from the LEA sector and those which are an additional cost to the exchequer. Their conclusions are as follows:

	2,000 schools	4,000 schools
Transfer Costs of Opting Out		
Annual Maintenance Grant	£377million	£754million
SPG (Development)	18.85m	37.7m
	£395.85m	£791.7m

	2,000 schools	4,000 schools
Additional Costs of Opting Out		
Capital Funding	£176.9m	£353.8m
Transitional Grant	103.5m	207.0m
SPG (Restructuring)	15.0m	30.0m
	£295.4m	£590.8m

Note: a number of items were not included in these totals, for example SPG for premises insurance and VAT.

As Bush and Coleman comment:

> The Conservative Party wants to secure a substantial increase in opting out but seems certain to experience tension between this policy aim and the need to control public expenditure. Favourable funding arrangements may be necessary to secure a large and successful autonomous sector but economic realities may mean that, in practice, GM schools will eventually be funded at the same level as those in the LEA sector.

Kenneth Clarke (the last but one Education Secretary) said that 'As the grant-maintained sector comes to predominate, there will not be any distinction in the capital provision.'[9]

Bush and Coleman observe that 'The Conservative government has deployed significant resources to support its political objective of creating an autonomous schools sector.' In other words, the initial financial advantage of GM schools was for the specific purpose of encouraging the spread of opting out. It is not sustainable in public expenditure terms - and, if the objective were realised, there would anyway be no need to sustain it (schools cannot, after all, opt back in). It is, in effect, a bait and, as we saw at the start of the chapter, it seems to be necessary: there is no evidence from experience that parents will vote for opting out without it (unless they do so to avoid a reorganisation proposal).

The inevitability of reductions in grants is not only

widely recognised; it is actually used in many schools as a reason for opting out quickly. It may be wiser to take time to explore the long-term and broader implications of the situation rather than rushing in because the bait looks attractive and others may get to it first, leaving less for those that follow later. The Chancellor of the Exchequer, Norman Lamont (speaking on a different financial issue to the European Policy Forum in July 1992) reminded his audience of an old Russian saying: 'Only mouse-traps have free cheese'.[10]

NOTES

1   *How to Become a Grant-Maintained School*, DES, 3rd Edition, January 1991.
2   *TES*, 11.1.91.
3   *Education*, 27.9.91.
4   *Guardian*, 25.9.91.
5   *Grant-Maintained Schools: Financial Arrangements*, DES, Circular 21/89.
6   *Guardian*, 7.8.91.
7   Brent Davies and Lesley Anderson, *Opting for Self Management*, Routledge, London 1992.
8   *The Financial Implications of Mass Opting Out*, Bush and Coleman, University of Leicester, 1992.
9   *Guardian*, 17.3.92.
10 Radio 4 News, 11 July 92.

7

THE PROCEDURES FOR OPTING OUT

Although essentially simple, and clearly explained in a DFE booklet, the procedures have defeated a number of governing bodies.[1] They are also open to abuse in both the spirit and the letter and, sadly, such abuse has been a feature in too many schools that have held opt out ballots; we shall return to this later. If a school does opt out, the governors become solely responsible for running it; it is, to say the least, unfortunate if the impression is given that even running the ballot properly is beyond them. It is a good idea if all concerned know exactly what is required.

All LEA maintained schools are eligible to apply for GM status except for nursery and special schools and those where closure proposals have already been agreed. The decision on whether or not to apply rests with the parents of registered pupils, who vote in a secret postal ballot arranged by the governing body and conducted by the Electoral Reform Society. There are two ways in which a ballot can be initiated: by far the more common is for the governing body to decide, by passing a resolution at a properly constituted meeting (for which the matter should appear on the agenda); this must be confirmed at a second meeting held between twenty-eight and forty-two days later. (The White Paper proposes to drop the requirement for a second meeting.) The LEA (and Trustees in the case of a voluntary school) must be consulted as soon as the first resolution is passed, in order that any views they wish to submit may be considered at the second meeting.

The other method is for parents at the school to present the governing body (through the chair or clerk) with a petition requesting a ballot. The petition must be signed by a number of parents equal to at least twenty per cent of the number of pupils registered at the school. (This could, therefore, be made up by two parents signing for each of just ten per cent of the pupils.)

On the passing of a second resolution, or receipt of a petition, it becomes the duty of the governing body to secure that a ballot is held. The LEA (and Trustees) must be notified at once in writing. The ballot must take place (ie. be completed) within three months of the governors' resolution or between twenty-eight days and two months plus twenty-eight days after receipt of the petition. The normal ballot period is three weeks (so, in fact, it is not actually possible to complete a ballot in as little as 28 days).

Every person recorded on the school's admission register as being a parent of a pupil is entitled to vote. The Act says that 'it shall be for the governing body to determine any question whether a person is a parent of a registered pupil at the school'. It is not only possible, but common, for there to be more than two 'parents' of a pupil (including, perhaps, the new partners of a child's separated natural parents). Each parent though, however many children they may have at the school, *has only one vote*. (Several ballots have had to be abandoned due to parents receiving a ballot paper for each of their children; the responsibility - and fault - in such cases lies squarely with the school, not the Electoral Reform Society.)

Parents have three explicit rights (in addition to their right to vote) connected with these procedures. (Whilst no explicit duty is placed on anyone to inform parents of these rights, the mere fact of their existence puts an implicit duty on the governing body to do so - and they certainly should.) Any parent of a registered pupil may:

> ask to inspect at the school (at any reasonable time and free of charge), a list containing the names and addresses of all parents (ERA 1988 Sec.60[7])

ask to be supplied with a copy of the list (Sec.60[7]),
for which they may be charged a fee not exceeding the
cost of supply (Sec.60[9])

ask (in writing) that their name should be excluded
from the list mentioned above (Sec.60[8]). (This does
not, of course, affect their right to vote.)

The rights to inspect, and receive a copy of, the list arise 'if
the request is made (a) in connection with any proposal that
a ballot should be held ... or (b) where the governing body
are under a duty ... to secure that such a ballot is held'
(Sec.60[7]).

The arrangements around the list of parents and
the rights described above have commonly given rise
to problems, sometimes through misunderstanding but
sometimes, undoubtedly, through wilfulness. The most
frequent problem is a refusal to supply a parent with a copy
of the list, which has led variously to the intervention of
DFE officials, consultation with solicitors and even a written
opinion from a barrister. The obvious reason for parents to
request the list and, presumably, the intention of Parliament
in giving that right, is to enable them to contact other
parents; the most obvious reason for refusing to supply the
list is to stop them. As these arrangements are central to the
conduct of the opt out procedures, it is worthwhile to clarify
the position.

The 'electoral register' for a ballot is the list of parents
that is sent to the Electoral Reform Society by the governing
body. The Act says that 'a person is eligible to vote ... if he
[*sic*] is (a) known to the governing body to be a parent of a
pupil registered at the school; and (b) named as a parent of
such a pupil in the register kept in accordance with the
requirements of the 1944 Act ... as that register has effect
on the day immediately following the end of the period
of fourteen days beginning with the date on which the
relevant resolution or request was passed or received by the

governing body' (Sec.61[14]). In other words, the electoral register closes fifteen days after the ballot has been initiated.

The right to inspect the list of parents during the first fourteen days is thus critical to ensuring that all the names of those who think they should be included actually are. The duty to maintain the list, it should be noticed, arises from the 1944 Act and is independent of opting out. A school's failure to have such a list is therefore no reason for even a delay in allowing parents to exercise their rights either to inspect the list or to be supplied with a copy (though it has certainly been used as such on a number of occasions). If a school does not have this list in good order, then the governing body has no business to embark on opting out procedures until it has remedied this deficiency.

The right of a parent not to have their name and address disclosed to others does present a problem, but there is a simple solution. The Act is clear that 'it shall be the duty of the governing body ... *at the request of any parent* ... to make available for inspection ... and to supply the parent with a copy of, a list containing the name and address of *every person* who is known to the governing body to be such a parent' (Sec.60[7]). Also that 'A governing body shall not disclose to a parent under subsection (7) above the name and address of any person *who has requested the governing body in writing* not to disclose that information' (note the tense: '*has requested*'). (Author's emphasis).

The only way to ensure that both rights are safeguarded is for parents to be made aware, in advance of opt out procedures ever being initiated, of the possibility of the list of parents at the school being made available to any parent, and of their right to notify the governing body in writing that they would not wish their details to be disclosed. The obvious time to do this is when a pupil is first registered, with a 'one-off' exercise to cover those that already are.

Once the arrangements for a ballot are sorted out, the

Electoral Reform Society (ERS) will send each voter a ballot paper, together with certain standard explanatory information. The ballot paper should be returned (a post-paid envelope is supplied) by the closing date - which must be consistent with the statutory time-table. If possible (and it is hard to see when it wouldn't be), the ballot should take place during term time.

There are a couple of pitfalls to avoid: a ballot held in the summer term will enable the parents of pupils about to leave to vote whilst excluding those of pupils due to start in September; even worse, a ballot initiated late in the summer term, but held in the autumn term, will exclude both groups - as the former's children will no longer be registered at the school, whilst the latter's children will not have been registered by the end of the period of fourteen days from either the governors' second resolution or the receipt of the petition. It is particularly aggravating for such parents to be excluded from a ballot that takes place after their children have started at the school; they will, after all, be the ones most affected by the outcome. The Department for Education booklet mentioned earlier issues a clear warning against this situation, describing it as 'clearly undesirable'. Parents may reflect on how accountable a governing body which ignores such advice is likely to be if it had complete control of a school's affairs.

The information supplied with the ballot paper consists of a general fact sheet about GM status (supplied to the ERS by the Department for Education) and a leaflet specific to the particular school (giving details of the proposed initial governing body, including their names and categories, and the proposed date of implementation for GM status). The fact sheet supplied by the DFE is available in a number of languages other than English, and the governing body should decide if it is appropriate to supply any of these as well. The information that accompanies the ballot paper must also be made available for every person employed at the school to inspect.

Only this factual information will be distributed by the ERS with the ballot paper. Material arguing the case for or against opting out may - and doubtless will - be sent to parents, but this must be separate. Many schools sending such information do so using either the school funds or even PTA-type funds; the propriety of doing so is questionable - especially if such funds are made available to express only one point of view. (The White Paper proposes to limit LEAs' spending on information for parents, and to give a grant to governing bodies to the value of the LEA limit. It is ironic that the Goverment should be so concerned about LEAs spending public funds to 'campaign against' opting out when, in reality, far more public money - coming from LEAs - is spent by schools persuading parents to opt out.)

The ballot paper now asks the question: 'Do You Wish (name) School to Apply for Grant-Maintained Status?' and there are two boxes, for a 'Yes' or 'No' response. (This simpler version replaced the original question, which was: 'Do you wish the governing body of your child's school to apply to the Secretary of State for Education and Science for grant-maintained status in accordance with Chapter IV of the Education Reform Act 1988?')

The ERS counts the votes and notifies the chair of governors and the DFE of the certified result, usually the day after the closing date. If more than fifty per cent of eligible parents have voted, the simple majority result is decisive; if fewer than fifty per cent vote, the result will be disregarded and a second ballot will be held at once, to be completed within fourteen days of the first result. The result of the second ballot is decisive regardless of the number of parents who vote.

It would obviously be unsatisfactory for such a major decision about the future of a school to rest on the views of a small proportion of parents. Whilst turnout is doubtless a factor which the Secretary of State considers in reaching his decision on whether or not to approve an application, it is desirable that as many parents as possible should vote. There are already several GM schools as a result of applications arising from second ballots, sometimes with low turnouts and a fairly narrow margin.

Bridgewater Hall and Brindley Hall, for example, (two schools which share the 'Stantonbury Campus' in Milton Keynes, Buckinghamshire and constitute, together, the largest comprehensive school in England) held ballots in very confused circumstances as a reaction to the threatened introduction of selection in the (all comprehensive) Milton Keynes area. The threat was never a very real one and, as it receded, what parental interest there was in opting out largely faded away. The first ballots in both schools failed to reach a fifty per cent turnout, but the second ballots attracted even fewer votes. The results were roughly a 60:40 'Yes' vote on turnouts little over thirty per cent. Both were approved for GM status by the Secretary of State, one with the positive support of twenty per cent of its parents, the other with nineteen per cent. Many parents (and neighbouring schools) felt that the whole situation had been used by a small group with an interest in opting out for their own ends - but it is a good illustration of the dangers of not using the opportunity to vote.

If the decisive ballot results in a 'No' vote, then no further ballot may be held for twelve months without the approval of the Secretary of State. If it results in a 'Yes' vote, then the governing body must, within six months of the result, publish detailed proposals for GM status and submit a copy to the Secretary of State.

The proposals must include:

the number of initial teacher and first (or foundation) governors

the name, address, category and term of office of

each initial governor

the arrangements for filling any vacancies in the elected (parent or teacher) categories

the name of the headteacher (who is a governor *ex-offico*)

the name under which it is proposed that the initial governing body will be incorporated

the arrangements for the admission of pupils, including the number it is proposed to admit in the September of or after incorporation

the provision for pupils with special educational needs

the arrangements for the induction of newly qualified teachers and the in-service training of teachers

the date of implementation of the proposals (incorporation date)

The proposals must be accompanied by a statement giving further details of the requirements affecting the governing body and must explain that within two months of their publication, any of the following may submit objections to the proposals to the Secretary of State:

any ten local government electors

the Trustees (if any) of the school concerned

the governing body of any school affected by the proposals

any local education authority concerned

Objections should be to the specific proposals, not to the principle of opting out.

The proposals must be displayed at or near any main entrance to the school and in at least one conspicuous place within the area served by the school. They must be made available for inspection at all reasonable times at the school or somewhere local to which the public has ready access (eg. a library). A notice must be published in at least one local paper containing a summary of the proposals, stating that they have been published and submitted to the Secretary of State for approval, saying where they may be inspected and explaining the opportunity to submit objections.

Once the two-month period for objections is expired, the Secretary of State may make a decision. He may reject the proposals, approve them without modification or, after consultation with the existing governing body, approve them with such modifications as he thinks desirable.

If the application is approved, the Secretary of State will give the new ('Initial') governing body of the GM school certain transitional powers related to the conduct of the school once it becomes incorporated; otherwise the school continues until then under the existing governing body. Transitional powers include such things as the appointment of staff, the arrangement and letting of contracts for services the school will require and the admission of pupils.

At the start of the chapter, reference was made to the procedures being open to abuse, in both the spirit and the letter. The problem of gaining access to the list of parents has already been covered, but there are broader issues to consider.

Opting out is a very major, and irrevocable, step; it will affect not only the present pupils and staff, but those to come in the future. It will also have an effect on other schools in the area, and across the LEA. One of the reasons that opting out is so contentious is that the decision on the transfer of a community asset from a democratically accountable body to the governors of the school itself rests in the hands only of those who happen to be using the asset at the time. It is as though, if public libraries were able to opt out to be run by a management committee (which could decide who could withdraw books, which books would be stocked, what the fines would be, etc., whilst the council - ie. local tax payers - went on paying for the service), the decision would rest with those who happened to have a book out *at the time*.

As we have seen, the Act unequivocally makes the decision on whether or not to apply to opt out a matter for parents, through a ballot. The governing body may decide to initiate a ballot, and it is hoped that governors and parents will take account of the views of the headteacher and staff - but the whole thrust of the political rhetoric surrounding the legislation, and the Act itself, make the issue one for parents.

In view of this, it is astonishing how frequently either governors or headteachers, or both together, have sought to control the procedures in such a way as to bring about the result that *they* want; it is also remarkable that they have got away with such manipulation so often - though, in some cases, the actions of heads and governors have been a major factor in provoking parents into the exactly opposite outcome.

A major weakness in the Act is the underlying assumption that parents have sufficient knowledge of how schools are financed and run to enable them to make an informed decision about a major change; most parents, in the author's experience, do not feel they have that knowledge. In that case they have only three choices: to seek the information, taking account of a range of views; to accept the information they are offered; or to make an uninformed decision. Some may choose not to make a decision, of course; many ballots have a disappointingly low turnout.

To a large extent, parents are dependent on the governors and/or head for the provision of information - because they control the means of communication in the school, as well as being in a position of influence and authority. They are often also in a position to control the whole process of debate leading up to a ballot. The role of heads was covered in Chapter 5 so, for now, we shall look at some examples - all based on experience - to illustrate the extremes of approach possible, and their likely consequences.

First, let us take the example of a school where, whatever their own views on the issue, governors and the head are primarily concerned with maintaining as consensual an approach as possible. There will probably be some discussion of opting out in the governing body; it is likely that more information will be sought for governors and maybe for staff - possibly with speakers invited to a meeting. Parents will be told that the issue is being looked at and will be invited to a meeting (preferably before a formal resolution is considered by the governing body) where, amongst others, a representative of the LEA will be invited to speak and answer questions. A variety of written information will be circulated, offering a range of perspectives and, in due course, a ballot will be held if that appears to be what people want.

In such an example, an openness of approach is evident; dissent from any prevailing view is accommodated; discussion is encouraged; time is given; resentment and division are minimised and, whatever the outcome, it is likely that a happy school will remain a happy school.

Second, an example of a school where the governors - or a dominant group of them - and the head wish the school to opt out. The issue may first surface as an agenda item for a governors' meeting. A number of (spurious) reasons will be given for the need for haste, the 'hidden agenda' being to minimise discussion, and thus opposition. A resolution will be moved to hold a ballot, and voted through by a majority. It is unlikely that speakers will be invited to any meetings (except, perhaps, the head of a GM school). Some literature (from the DFE and the GMS Centre/Choice in Education)[2] may be provided, otherwise information will be given by governors who have 'gone into it' and believe (wrongly) that they know all they - or anyone else - needs to know about it. Staff may not even be consulted (unless some senior members are known to be in favour), and staff ballots will be discouraged.

A timetable for the procedures will be set which is as close as practicable to the statutory minimum; the period until the (inconveniently) necessary (at present) second governors' meeting may even coincide with a holiday period (if everything has been thought through before raising the issue!). A parents' meeting will be discouraged, but 'surgeries' may be arranged for individual year groups with selected governors (anything to keep parents from getting together, and allowing opposition to develop in an organised way). If unavoidable, a meeting will be held (perhaps after the ballot has begun) - then at least no-one will be able to say the school wasn't open - but the platform of speakers will be far from balanced.

Parents will be sent 'information' that paints an exaggerated picture of the benefits opting out would bring the school, and their children. It will dwell on finance, especially the number of extra staff the school could employ. It won't mention the possibility of raising salaries (and will specifically avoid mentioning any possibility of raising the head's salary).

Anyone seeking further information, requesting outside speakers with an alternative perspective or, worst of all, asking for a copy of the list of parents, will be treated as eccentric, potentially difficult or a confirmed trouble-maker. This makes parents feel particularly vulnerable, since they often feel it may affect the school's attitude to their children. If all goes according to plan, the ballot will proceed reasonably smoothly; parents will bow, relatively unquestioningly, to the wisdom of those better placed to decide - and will deliver the desired result.

That may sound dreadfully cynical; it is. However, it is a pattern that would be recognised by a great many governors, staff and parents amongst the schools which have been through the process. But sometimes, it doesn't work.

In many cases, a school which is accustomed to an autocratic style of leadership merely goes through the motions of confirming its lot. Little changes; the increased opportunities for autocracy to flourish will barely be noticed where it is already rampant.

In others, all hell breaks loose! Having become accustomed to the rhetoric of 'parent power', many resent being treated as 'voting fodder'; some even know their rights, or find out about them, and expect to be able to exercise them; they speak to others and find they are not alone in their views. Some are anxious about the broader implications, especially the effects on other schools - where they may have younger children. Some have social consciences and some (horror of horrors) are politically motivated (it is axiomatic that opting out is *not* a political issue). When such people get together, especially if they discover that some governors and staff share their reservations, they grow in confidence, they organise their own meetings; they circulate their own literature - and sometimes they discover (as do the governing body and head) that they have become the majority.

Whatever the outcome in the second type of school, it is not a very positive experience. Repression is either demonstrably sustained, or people break out - in which case it will take a while for the dust to settle (although the long-term result may be beneficial).

For our last example, let us consider a school where the governors and head do not agree. The only opportunity either has to out-manoevre the other is by, covertly, encouraging a group of parents to organise a petition requiring the governing body to hold a ballot. It is not usually difficult to find a few parents to take a petition around at the school gate, or in a meeting of some sort.

Unfortunately, it is also very easy to get other parents to sign it without even reading what it actually says, and Local Schools Information has frequently received complaints that parents were misled about the nature of such petitions (they are often told it is a petition 'to request more information on opting out', or 'to get more money for the school'). However, there is no redress in such situations; never sign anything without reading it first! Many of the parents' petitions that have been used to require a ballot appear to have been inspired by heads or governors, but when the petition is presented, everyone's hands are clean! From there on, the matter will be dealt with in one of the ways above or - as in most schools that have been through the opting out process - by some middle way between the two extremes: some damage will be done, to relationships in and around the school, but it will usually be manageable and temporary. Whether or not it will be worthwhile may take some years to judge.

NOTES

1   *How to Become a Grant-Maintained School*, DES.
2   See Chapter 3 on the Political Background to opting out for details of these bodies.

8

THE CHANGING ROLE
OF LEAs

It has often been said that if LEAs didn't exist, they would have to be invented; presumably that is why they were. However there are also those that think they are no longer required: Bob Balchin, chair of the Grant-Maintained Schools Foundation, said that '[the] White Paper means that the end of local authority control of education is now in sight'.[1] LEAs have been mentioned, inevitably, on almost every page, so here we shall look specifically at what they are, what they do, how they are changing - and whether we do still need them.

LEA stands for Local Education Authority; in other words, the local authority (council) that has responsibility for the provision of education in an area. In metropolitan areas that is the Metropolitan District Councils (in London it is the local Borough Councils, the City of Westminster and City of London Councils). Elsewhere it is the County Councils, though these are currently the subject of a review of local government structures that will lead to further changes over the next few years. The Isles of Scilly have a unique local government arrangement, which includes responsibility for education. The total number of LEAs in England and Wales is one hundred and seventeen.

It is a strange feature of the service that councils are almost invariably referred to, in the educational context, as 'LEAs' rather than 'councils' - as if they were somehow a different thing. (The only authority to have been responsible solely for education was the Inner London Education Authority (ILEA) - which was abolished by the 1988 Act, giving that responsibility to the inner London boroughs.)

135

Historically, education departments have been by far the largest department within councils, accounting for around half of the total budget and workforce. This may have contributed to the fact that they often have an identity somewhat distinct from other areas of council work, although councils' provision in other areas certainly affects educational opportunity (eg. housing and social services). However, relationships between departments have had to change rapidly as a result of a number of recent changes in the law, especially the introduction of Compulsory Competitive Tendering (CCT) for certain services and the increasing autonomy of schools as a result of LMS and opting out. Client/contractor relationships are becoming far more widespread, and even where schools purchase the services of other departments through the agency of the education department, they are far more aware of the costs of these services. We shall look shortly at the ways in which councils are accommodating these changes, but first we shall consider the range of functions of LEAs.

A number of councils have produced leaflets for parents, describing the role and function of the LEA; one recent example, from a large Conservative-controlled county council, listed the services it offers under six headings:

Pupils and Students: provision for those with special needs; transport; grants and awards; county sports teams, orchestras and drama festivals; careers advice; help for the gifted; outdoor education centres; school meals.

Parents: information about schools; school admissions; complaints and appeals; advice on grants and awards.

Governors: training; professional advice and information; financial services and advice; legal advice; discussion forums; insurance.

Schools: local, and immediate, advice and support; legal advice; financial advice, including audit; staff recruitment; structural building maintenance; monitoring and inspection; personnel services; school meals; caretaking and cleaning; payroll; insurance scheme for long-term teacher absence; capital building work; training for administrators; central purchasing; publications on good practice; grounds maintenance.

Teachers: Training, especially for new curriculum developments; Learning Resource Service; Library Service; Teachers' centres; countywide teacher associations; Academic Councils; advice on assessment; professional counselling; teacher appraisal; maintaining employment opportunities.

The Community: adult education; youth service; support for the arts; pre-school education.

Some authorities offer a smaller range, some offer more, but all provide services that are generally appreciated by those that use them. One of the reasons that such activities are not more widely recognised is that they remain largely 'invisible' to those who do not come into direct contact with them. It is not uncommon to hear teachers describe as invaluable or even essential an aspect of a LEA's support services of which most parents - and even many governors - may be largely unaware. If present services (already much reduced by budget cuts over recent years) are to be preserved in some form then the community as a whole must be made more aware of their existence and value. It is very much harder to replace something than to remove it.

In addition to the services they offer, LEAs perform a number of strategic functions, such as deciding on the overall level of expenditure on education, planning for overall levels of provision, liaising with many other bodies (from central government to local employers), and many more. Some of their activities are statutory requirements; others may be desirable, but will be limited by the resources available. Tower Hamlets Education Department produced a document listing the statutory duties of a LEA, which it numbered at seventy-three.[2] They include the provision of schooling and support to schools and individuals; the regulation of that provision; the supply of a variety of information, advice and training; the administration of appeals procedures; the establishment of health and safety policies and procedures; the inspection of premises and a host of others. Some already no longer apply as a result of changes in the law, which are bringing about a substantial change in the role of LEAs.

As we have already seen, responsibility for (state) schools is divided between the Secretary of State (central government), LEAs and the governing bodies of schools - and the balance between them has shifted a great deal recently, and is still changing - albeit more slowly now. Central government has largely determined, through the National Curriculum, what is to be taught in schools and is also seeking to influence how it is taught; it also indirectly controls expenditure. The essential planning function of LEAs is being largely replaced by market forces, though they remain responsible for ensuring that provision is made for all those entitled to it (both by building new schools, should there be a need for more places, and by making provision for those who, for whatever reason, are not attending school); the administration of the service is being increasingly delegated to schools themselves, although the LEA continues to provide support and a range of services. GM schools (and, as a result of the Further and Higher Education Act 1992, FE and sixth-form colleges and centres) are no longer part of their responsibility, though they retain duties towards some pupils in them. The Schools Act 1992, whilst placing new duties on LEAs to collect and publish information (league tables) about schools, altered (very controversially) the arrangements for the inspection of schools, largely removing another key function of LEAs.

All in all, then, the role of LEAs is nearing the end of a

pretty major series of changes - yet the role that remains, or even remains to be created, for them is still not clearly defined. There are obvious reasons for this. The Government has published an extraordinary number of separate pieces of legislation (sixteen Education Acts and many more affecting local government) since 1979 - some of them contradictory or, at least, requiring further changes to earlier changes (often before the earlier ones were fully implemented); it even changed the name of the Department from the Dept. of Education and Science (DES) to the Dept. For Education (DFE) within six months of its move to new headquarters, requiring changes to its own recently changed stationery! Yet in all this, there has been no clear policy on LEAs themselves; the many changes have been incidental and/or piecemeal. The Education Reform Act 1988 runs to two hundred and eighty-four pages, with two hundred and thirty-eight sections and thirteen schedules - not one on the reform of LEAs.

LEAs themselves have adapted as they went along - they have had to. Some have done so faster and some better than others - but none has yet been able to plan and put into practice a comprehensive new approach to its own role and function because of the uncertainty that remains as a result of the vacuum in central government policy (even the position over the re-organisation of local government is confusing and the proposals in the White Paper do not constitute a clear vision of the position of LEAs: some new powers are proposed, while others are removed - and the paper acknowledges that the situation will vary around the country). In any case, authorities have been fully occupied with implementing the deluge of change that they have had to cope with. Now, however, there is light at the end of the tunnel. It seems likely that there will be little (if any) education legislation for some time after the forthcoming Bill is enacted, so LEAs will be able to take stock and assess their new position in the light of their remaining functions and resources. They will then be able to tailor their internal arrangements to match what is required, in line with their own policies. It remains to be seen if the light is really the end of the tunnel, or if it is an approaching train that will sweep them into oblivion; that will depend, in part, on the extent to which the GM sector expands and the proposals in the White Paper (which will form the basis of the new Bill) become implemented. This, in turn, will largely depend on the success with which authorities themselves identify and perform a role which schools and the public - their clients - perceive as still desirable or even essential. The process of reorganisation needs to be undertaken urgently - and is well under way in many authorities.

The task facing LEAs is to develop and project a vision of their future role to replace the image of their past. They must also devise a strategy for putting it into practice as quickly as possible, and 'sell' their vision to those whom they serve before other events overtake them. The objective, of course, is not to protect the position of LEAs as Town and County Hall-based empires (an image much promoted by hostile politicians and others) but to protect the provision of a coherent education service which meets the needs and aspirations of the whole community - locally and nationally. The great strength of a democratically accountable basis for such provision is that there is a mechanism for assessing those needs and aspirations, for distributing resources in a way which reflects them and for responding to the local community as a whole. The dangers in a market-led, or government-appointed, alternative is that the basis of provision is less clear; the system is less responsive (except to 'buying power') and many may find their needs unmet - with little or nothing they can do about it.

There are two distinct, but related, questions that arise in considering public service provision: first, what services/functions is it necessary or desirable to provide, for

140

both institutions and individuals? Second, who is able to provide them - and what factors are important in deciding which of the possible providers is the most appropriate or desirable? The simple answer to what is it necessary to provide is supplied by the list of (current) statutory requirements; however, there will be a variety of opinions on what additional provision is desirable - which will, anyway, be limited by the availability of resources. The second question is harder to answer.

The Government has systematically, and with some success across a range of public services, challenged the notion that existing/traditional providers (in this case, councils) are the only possible source of provision; it has been less successful in convincing people that, in many cases, they are not the most desirable/appropriate source. There is not space here to go into great detail on the issue of public service provision; there is more than enough that could be said on the subject to make a book on its own, and it has probably already been written. However, there are some points that are worth making.

Perhaps the most important factor, which really overrides other considerations, is that of democracy. Democracy is not often given great prominence in these discussions, nor is it accorded great understanding; this is strange given how much - in an abstract sense - we are said to value it, and how indignant we become when it is denied or abused elsewhere in the world. Since 1979, Conservative governments have made a great many changes which have shifted power, and accountability, away from elected local authorities and into the hands of central government (we have already looked at some examples affecting education and local government spending, and there are many more); government-appointed bodies have increasingly assumed responsibility for public services, and the White Paper proposes to extend this trend dramatically in education. The Government claims it is giving people more choice by giving institutions (such as schools and hospitals) more power and responsibility, thus making them more accountable; but democracy goes much deeper than choice - and choice is often more of an illusion than a reality.

Public services are resources available to the population as a whole, paid for out of public funds and provided or overseen by a public body, democratically accountable in some way. The idea of 'no taxation without representation' is still more or less valid and universally supported - at least rhetorically. However, the extent to which people fail to make the connection between their general commitment to democracy and the process of making decisions about concrete reality is demonstrated by the frequency with which one hears it said that 'politics should be kept out of education'. Politics is simply the process of government: what should be provided; for whom; by whom; at what cost; who should pay, and how much; and so on. Party politics is the manner in which that process is organised, with different parties promoting, and seeking support for, their way of governing; their policies and priorities. We tend to take a dim view of one-party states and dictatorships, whilst cheerfully staying away in droves from our own elections - especially local government elections (despite the fact that these affect education, housing, social services, leisure and recreation facilities, highways, environmental health, trading standards, refuse collection, street cleaning and lighting, planning, etc.).

Whoever makes the provision - in this case, of education services - most of us would wish to have some say in how our money is spent; not only on what, and on whom, it is spent - but on the quality and value provided. It is clear that a range of organisations, or even individuals, may be capable of *performing* a service, but responsibility for *providing* public services must rest with either central or local government if accountability is to be preserved. It seems logical that the greatest accountability lies closest to the point of delivery - which is, after all, the principle underlying devolution of responsibility to institutions.

This brings us to the dilemma at the heart of this matter: if power and responsibility are removed from locally elected bodies and passed to even more local, but unelected, bodies overseen by central government, does this enhance or diminish accountability? In the case of a school, for example, it may be argued that GM status increases responsiveness to its users (pupils and parents) by giving it control of all its resources, and removing the influence of LEA policies - but is it more accountable? How do those who contribute to its funding, but do not (though may in future) have a child at the school exert any influence at all? What does a parent do who can't get their child admitted - or whose child is expelled? We have already looked (in Chapter 4) at the accountability of GM schools to parents, and shall return to the issue of choice in the closing chapters.

So, the choice over responsibility for *providing* public services lies between a local council and some other body, answerable to the government. The choice over *performing* such services is potentially much wider. If there is a statutory duty on a council to provide a particular service/function, then one way of ensuring that it is available is for the council to provide it itself. This also enhances control over quality. Where alternative sources are readily available, the council may choose to purchase the service elsewhere (a good example of this choice is home to school transport, which - for those entitled to it - may be provided by the council's own vehicles, by a contractor hired by the council or by passes purchased by the council for use on normal public transport). In such a case, key criteria for deciding who is to perform a service will include cost, efficiency and quality - an aspect of which will be safety.

It may be that other factors are also important, such as

whether contractors employ local people or whether their employment practices are good. In both these examples, such considerations may have a significant effect on the well-being of the local community which, in turn, may affect the level of demand for (and therefore cost of) support such as social services.

Some services, for which there is no commercial demand outside the public sector, are unlikely to exist within the private sector, where profit is the main motive, but may be available within the voluntary sector, which covers a host of provision, but depends largely on public funds in some form for its survival. One danger in the process of removing either the power or financial ability of local authorities to perform services is that the private sector is unlikely to find the provision of a comprehensive range of services attractive or profitable, so some may disappear altogether. This, too, is considered further in the following chapters.

There have been several contributions to the discussion of what the LEA of the future will do, and how. The Audit Commission (the independent government watch-dog which investigates the provision of, and expenditure on, public services but, incidentally, was refused the power to oversee the GM school sector) described the role of LEAs after the 1988 Act as:

> a leader, articulating a vision of what the education service is trying to achieve;
>
> a partner, supporting schools ... and helping them to fulfil this vision;
>
> a planner of facilities for the future;
>
> a provider of information to the education market, helping people to make informed choices;
>
> a regulator of quality in schools ...;
>
> a banker, channelling the funds which enable local institutions to deliver.[3]

More recently, Howard Davis, then Controller of the Audit Commission, wrote that, whilst much of this remained valid, local authorities needed to review their position as the government's attitude to them had hardened:

> I would (now) put the regulator function first, and would link it more closely to the notion of the authority as the advocate of consumer interests. I would emphasise that the authority was the buyer of education on the citizen's behalf. And I would put it firmly within the twin frameworks of the purchaser/provider split and of the Citizen's Charter.[4]

Joan Sallis, president of the Campaign for the Advancement of State Education (CASE), writing on the pitfalls of an extension of opting out in the run up to the publication of the White Paper, highlighted the role of the LEA in overseeing the probity of school management:

> The whole idea of self-managing schools could lose its heady excitement and backfire on politicians if even the slightest suspicion persists that they are not being managed in an open, fair and accountable way. The local authority, at present the bobby on the beat, would then not seem such a dull plodder after all.[5]

A key aspect of the role of LEAs in the past, though now diminished, is that of 'developer and innovator'. When critics, including ministers, accuse LEAs of 'interfering' in the work of schools, they generally refer to initiatives with which they disagree. More polite terms are applied to developments which find favour, and a great many - indeed most - educational initiatives arise from the policies of LEAs. LMS itself was a LEA development, as were records of achievement, business/school compacts and the model for intervention in 'failing schools' now apparently favoured by the Prime Minister - the latter three introduced and developed by the ILEA, abolished by the 1988 Act. If other LEAs were to meet the same end, it is hard to see where such beneficial developments would arise; schools, of course, contribute a great deal, but generally lack the resources, both financial and human, to do so beyond a limited level - even on a co-operative basis.

A great many schools (perhaps the vast majority) are, anyway, distinctly uncomfortable about the extent of the trend towards increased competition, rather than co-operation, between schools. This is generally not through anxiety about their own viability, but because of a genuine - and often deeply held - conviction that raising educational standards and improving the level of provision for the majority of pupils is best achieved co-operatively. A degree of competition does bring benefits, but there is widespread concern over the development of a two-tier system that seems the inevitable consequence of the rigid application of market principles. Whilst most heads, governors and parents feel under pressure to avoid being relegated to a lower tier, there is a strong commitment to preserving, and being part of, a coherent system of provision that meets the needs of all. LEAs played a crucial role in laying the basis for co-operation between schools, which would be further undermined by an increase in opting out.

Perhaps the most critical role of LEAs at the present time is to harness co-operative feelings and facilitate as far as possible the development of schools in a direction that does preserve coherence. To this end, it is essential that schools are drawn into a dialogue about the nature of the present change and the mechanism for managing it, rather than being left to arrive at their own conclusions from a position of isolation and, possibly, increasing mutual suspicion. Heads, staff and governors are looking for support; parents are looking for information. LEAs are uniquely placed to provide both.

The marked shift in the distribution of powers between central government, local authorities and governing bodies (which are greatly influenced by headteachers) must be recognised. New ways of working, and delivering the education service in schools, must be offered and it must obviously be acknowledged that schools that are dissatisfied with what is on offer may decide to opt out, with inevitable consequences for other schools in the area.

Whilst education departments will undoubtedly take the lead in this exercise - consulting their schools and others about it - other departments should also be as involved in the planning stage, as they will have to be in the implementation stage if the strategy is to be successful. The LMS Initiative, an independent national body bringing together a wide range of professional and consumer interests, commissioned a study of the implementation of LMS in England and Wales from the National Foundation for Educational Research and Coopers & Lybrand Deloitte (one of the large firms of consultants increasingly being used by the government, local authorities and others). Their report emphasised the need for managers of council departments besides education to share, to a much greater extent, an awareness of the implications of LMS:

> The potential impact of schools leaving the authority ('opting out') because they are dissatisfied with services, or remaining with the authority but deciding not to purchase services, is considerable given the size of the schools' budget within the local authority. This means that the development of the local authority's strategy for LMS [and, of course, opting out] is a collective responsibility for all Chief Officers and their departments, and one in which the Chief Executive may wish to play a leading role.[6]

This may require an acceleration in the evolution of relationships between council departments mentioned earlier, but survival depends on the ability to adapt.

Another document prepared by Coopers & Lybrand for the School Management Task Force within the Department for Education, based on a study of best practice in a sample of schools, says:

> Schools have always taken buying decisions. But what is new is

147

the range of services for which they will now need to make
decisions and the size of the budgets involved... The response of
most LEAs will be to offer arrangements to heads and governors
which allow schools to buy back the services they received
previously. But this also raises the possibility of schools buying
back a higher or lower level of service and of investigating what is
available from other providers... The natural provider of most
services to any school is the school's own LEA and this will
continue for as long as the school finds the services to be of good
quality and value for money.[7]

LEAs are increasingly offering schools a range of services, at
a range of levels and costs, to meet their needs. Such
arrangements are called 'service level agreements'. With
increasing levels of budget delegation to schools, they offer
almost all the advantages claimed for GM status with the
added benefits of remaining within what some authorities
have described as 'the LEA family' of schools. As we shall
see in Chapter 10, the alternative for schools which opt
out is to seek the provision they need from the private
sector - where the guiding principle is return on investment;
service to the public is a consideration only in as much as it
generates a profit.

NOTES

1   *The Times*, 30.7.92.
2   *Statutory Duties of the Local Education Authority*, Tower
    Hamlets Education Department, 1991.
3   *Losing an Empire, Finding a Role: the LEA of the Future*,
    The Audit Commission, 1989.
4   *TES*, 2.8.91.
5   *Independent*, 21.5.92.
6   *Local Management in Schools: A Study into Formula Funding &
    Management Issues*, Coopers & Lybrand Deloitte, 1992.
7   *Buying for Quality*, DFE 1992.

9

THE EXTENSION OF OPTING OUT

Although the White Paper refers to the 'rapid and successful growth in the number of grant-maintained schools', when it was published at the end of the school year in July 1992, four years after opting out had become possible, the position was as follows (remember, there are nearly 25,000 eligible schools, and 117 LEAs):

Ballots	558 in 85 LEAs
'Yes' votes	434
'No' votes	124
GM schools operating:	219 in 54 LEAs
GM status approved:	67 in 21 LEAs
	(inc. 5 additional LEAs)
GM status rejected:	47

Note: the remainder of those voting to opt out are still 'in the pipe-line'.

Political control of LEA	No. of Ballots	GM schools operating	GM schools approved
Conservative	357	151	50
Labour	92	30	4
Lib-Dem	7	6	0
No Overall Control	102	32	13

There were only nineteen LEAs where the number of ballots held was in double figures, fifteen of them under Conservative control. Between them, these nineteen (16 per cent of the 117 LEAs) accounted for 375 (67 per cent) of the total number of ballots. In 32 LEAs there had still been no ballot at all. Thus, far from being a national phenomenon, opting out is heavily concentrated in a small number of authorities, mostly in the south-east and home counties.

Between the April general election (when it became clear that GM schools had a secure future, at least for the next few years) and the end of July 1992, there were 95 ballots. Despite the Conservative victory and the consequent predictions of a torrent of schools opting out, this was 30 fewer than in the same period in the previous year. Furthermore, in nine cases, fewer than 50 per cent of eligible parents voted, so second ballots were required. The results of these ballots demonstrated that the issue of opting out remained very open.

In twelve of the 86 decisive ballots (which included four second ballots where the turnout was still below 50 per cent), parents voted against opting out; in 43, the proportion of eligible parents voting 'Yes' was below 50 per cent. Sixty of the 86 were in the nineteen LEAs where the number of ballots held is in double figures, and the number of LEAs where there has still been no ballot has only dropped from 36 to 32 in the period since February 1992. Thus, parents are still showing little general enthusiasm for opting out, and there is no evidence of opting out spreading very much beyond the few areas where it is concentrated.

Disquiet has been expressed on a number of occasions within Conservative Party circles at the lack of progress on opting out, particularly in the run-up to the General Election. The influential Carlton Club produced a paper in 1991 arising from an 'investigative seminar' 'to assist the Chairman of the Party, Central Office Management and the Ministerial Team plus their advisers, in both their deliberations plus formulation of a policy statement, combined with an action plan to be placed before the electorate pre and post the next General Election.'[1] Amongst those contributing or present were: the (then) Schools Minister, Michael Fallon; Malcolm Thornton MP (Chair, Parliamentary Select Committee on Education); David Hart (Gen. Sec. National Association of Headteachers); Robert Balchin (Chair, Grant-Maintained Schools Foundation) and

Donald Naismith (Director of Education, LB Wandsworth). The seminar was chaired by Sir Norman Fowler MP, who has since become the Chairman of the Conservative Party. This, then, was no obscure 'think-tank', the output of which can be lightly dismissed as well outside the mainstream.

The Carlton Club paper observed that the Government would be judged, in part, on its performance over education and that 'It must be recognised there is mounting concern that Conservatives' reforms have yet to produce results'. Having expressed disappointment over the slow progress of opting out, the paper criticised the Government for under-estimating the hostility to the policy 'predominantly from socialist authorities ... [but] a marked degree of opposition came also from Tory authorities', and also for over-estimating the leadership and management qualities of many headteachers, though it conceded that heads 'have been confronted with over-expectations of what savings can be achieved by a GM school'.

The paper recommended a number of changes which have subsequently been broadly adopted by the Government in the White Paper. These were: to limit spending to a fixed amount by both sides during the 'debate' process; to simplify and shorten the ballot procedure; to enable primary schools to opt out in groups (the paper said 'It is clear that smaller primary schools will not be able to cope alone as GM schools'); to remove restrictions on schools which would prefer to change their educational style and type to become grammar schools, City Technology Colleges or Magnet Schools (ie. schools which specialise in a particular subject); and to introduce Regional Educational Boards to manage the educational system.

The paper also said that, 'A radical review of the disproportionate influence of the Church and charitable trusts in the administration of the education system was considered long overdue', a view with which the new Secretary of State, John Patten, who is a Catholic, plainly

151

disagrees: the White Paper conspicuously acknowledges and welcomes the role of the Churches in schools. The Government was recommended to 'take urgent steps to curtail and diminish the influence and power ... of large numbers of educationalists ... (who), with few honourable exceptions, are perceived as the Achilles heel of our education system', a suggestion that many observers would suggest has been followed by successive Conservative governments in recent years - especially through government appointments on a number of key education bodies. Paradoxically, the paper also urged greater power for headteachers: 'The Government has: placed too much power in the hands of governors ... Headteachers should have responsibility for: Staffing; The Curriculum; Procurement; Management to a Budget.'

A key section of the document dealt with the approach to LEAs as the GM sector expands:

> A fundamental question which arises out of the scheme to introduce GM schools is whether these schools should be given complete autonomy to run their own affairs: If so, should LEAs be abolished because they are, in effect, redundant and obsolete? ... Allowing [LEAs] to pass away as part of the wider reorganisation of local government planned by the Conservatives is considered the best way forward. At the same time, the Investigative Seminar strongly counselled the Conservative Government against adopting a 'head-on ' confrontational approach on this emotive issue and recommends instead that [LEAs] should merely be allowed to pass away and 'wither on the vine'

It is interesting to observe the extent to which the Carlton Club seminar's ideas have been taken up. The Government is plainly hoping for an acceleration in the rate of opting out through its White Paper proposals, which include: moves to limit LEA spending during the 'debate' process; dropping the requirement for a second governors' resolution prior to a ballot; provision to permit primary schools to opt out in groups; and an extension of variety by allowing GM schools to change their nature. There is also a proposal to create a

Funding Agency for Schools, which could establish regional offices, to oversee the GM sector and take over functions from LEAs as the number of GM schools increases. A head-on confrontation over the future of LEAs has been avoided in favour of allowing them to 'wither on the vine', if parents can be persuaded to opt out in greater numbers. However, there is also a proposal to establish 'Education Associations' to take over 'failing schools' from their governing bodies and LEAs and either improve them, in which case they would become grant-maintained without any parents' ballots, or close them. All these ideas are examined in the next chapter.

The Department for Education document for governors of GM schools[2] (described in Chapter 4) seeks, through advice on their conduct, to restore the balance in favour of heads to some extent, but no changes in the powers of heads and governors were proposed in the White Paper (though it was proposed that the Secretary of State would have power to replace any or all of the First Governors of a GM school). It is hard to see how the notion of accountability, and particularly the emphasis previously given to the importance of parent governors, can be squared with a transfer of power to headteachers. However, there is growing pressure (reported in the *TES* of 24 July 1992) from GM heads to curb the power of governors:

> Heads of more than half the current 250 grant-maintained schools have privately told ministers that over-powerful governors are jeopardising their attempts to raise standards. Their paper, intended to influence the content of the White Paper, says: 'Regrettably, in a small minority of schools, governing bodies have sought to apply a degree of day-to-day control which ignores the head's leadership role and which prevents effective and efficient management'.

The GM heads are unlikely to abandon their quest for changes, and a group of them have set up the Association of Heads of Grant-Maintained Schools, in addition to the 'official' Standing Advisory Committee for Grant-Maintained Schools, through which the Department for Education consults the schools.

One of the founder members of the Association, Eamonn Harris (Head of Queen Elizabeth Boys School, Barnet) has views on parental choice of school and accountability of heads with which many would disagree, but which illustrate the problems and uncertainties of the position in the GM sector. As reported in *Education* (14 August 1992):

> He believes he is in the mainstream of Government thinking, and nothing in the White Paper proves him wrong... he told me that the requirement in the 1944 Education Act to find a school place for all children should be abandoned. Parents alone should be responsible for finding school places. If they fail to co-operate properly with the school, and cause their children to be expelled, their children should not be educated... He interviews prospective parents very carefully, asking many searching questions. If they are not suitable he persuades them to go elsewhere. Once at the school, they must do what he considers to be their duty, or their sons will have to leave... If Mr Harris gets his way, and LEAs are abolished, along with the duty to find a school place for all children, the problem will be solved. Parents who want their children to be educated will have to dance to the tune of heads like Mr Harris.

It should now be clear that any substantial extension of opting out would bring about considerable changes to the present system of school provision, many of which would affect not only pupils but also their parents and others in the community - including prospective and future parents. The nature of some of these changes is already apparent; others are still subject to speculation, and therefore the exercise of judgement. These are key matters for debate in arriving at any consensual view of the best way forward, which we shall consider in the final chapter. Here, partly by way of summary of what has been covered already, we shall consider briefly the main areas of obvious, or likely, change that would arise as a result of such an extension.

The role of LEAs has already been diminished and would be further eroded, or maybe eliminated, by widespread opting out. Market forces would increasingly replace strategic planning as the mechanism for change - though some strategic overview and control will always be required. The creation of a government appointed body for this purpose is proposed, the powers of which would be extended as necessary. A number of existing services which do not lend themselves to earning a profit, particularly those meeting the needs of minority (but not wealthy) groups, may diminish or disappear as a result of the withdrawal of LEA funds and the privatisation of services. (Music, art, drama, outdoor education, remedial teaching support, provision for ethnic minority groups and a variety of specialist teachers' centres would be particularly vulnerable.)

Opting out has created problems for the planning of school provision. Opening new schools, knowing they might soon opt out, is not an attractive proposition for LEAs, but the far more common problem of closing schools has been made a great deal harder. Since 1988, over one hundred schools facing unwelcome re-organisation proposals have attempted to opt out - and more than forty have succeeded. The rate of removal of surplus places (costing, remember, at least £750 million a year) has plummeted. According to the *Guardian* (20 July 1992), 'The number of secondary schools affected by local reorganisations fell by 71 per cent - from 612 in 1987, the year before the first opt out ballots, to 174 in 1991 ... The Government, in a parliamentary answer to Derek Fatchett, said 43 reorganisation schemes, involving different numbers of schools, were rejected because of applications being made for grant-maintained status'.

There is a widespread feeling that the present mechanism for funding even LEA schools, let alone GM

155

schools, will lead to the creation of a 'two-tier' state school system. Whilst there have always been differences between schools, they now seem set to become greater rather than smaller. (It would in fact be a three-tier system, of course, because the private sector - which is supported financially by the tax-payer through charitable status and the assisted places scheme - is mostly far better resourced than any state school.)

The process of transfer from primary to secondary school seems likely to become increasingly chaotic as parents apply separately to any (or all) of the GM schools in their area, and possibly, through the LEA, to its schools as well. Popular schools need some method of selection to decide which pupils to admit; as more of them opt out, and gain control of their own admissions policies and arrangements, selection by academic ability or 'aptitude' (as often - if, perhaps, unlawfully - tested by interview, of pupils and parents) will spread. At the same time, the independence of appeal procedures will diminish - leaving increasing numbers of parents frustrated. The net effect on choice will probably be uneven but, again, disadvantaged groups are likely to find their problems compounded and their opportunities restricted.

And what will anyone who is dissatisfied with any aspect of the situation be able to do about it? If parents have a problem with a GM school their child attends, they will have to take it up with the governing body. If that does not resolve it, they will have to approach the Secretary of State. Their chances of success will probably depend on how widely their problem is shared by other parents, because the only real sanction they have - that of exercising 'choice' and moving their child to another school - is so disruptive for the child that most would regard it as a last resort; for many it would probably never be a realistic option. The school would only be vulnerable, and hence necessarily accountable, if a significant number of parents were dissatisfied; otherwise the headteacher and governors are broadly free to react as they wish.

If parents have problems getting their children into (or having them excluded from) GM schools, much the same difficulty arises. It is inevitable that, if opting out spreads to a significant number of schools, these issues will become commonplace. Such situations arise constantly with schools, and LEAs - through both elected local councillors and authority officers - play a major role in sorting them out. In the GM sector, there are no such opportunities.

To set against these disadvantages (actual or potential) there needs to be some major benefit to be derived from opting out if it is to be extended widely.

The Government's declared position has always been that the introduction of greater competition between schools - to which it sees opting out as the key - is for the purpose of raising educational standards across the board. However, there is, as yet, no evidence to support this position. By February 1992, HM Inspectors had spent a total of three hundred days in GM schools;[3] they spent more than twenty days in each of five individual schools - yet not a single report on their findings has been published, and there is apparently no intention to publish one yet.

This really is most peculiar: a major - and radical - educational reform, designed (we are told) to raise the level of performance in schools throughout the system is subjected to a higher level of scrutiny by HMI than that applied to schools generally, *yet not a word of their findings is made public.* It is all the more remarkable since, throughout that period, parents have been strongly encouraged to support a widespread extension of the reform - possibly to the extent that it replaces the system that has operated for almost the last fifty years - *without a shred of evidence that it is achieving its objective.*

There have been a number of occasions in recent years when it has suited the Government's purpose to publish, and publicise, a report from HMI; in some cases it has been done with breath-taking speed. Had HMI found evidence that opting out *does* bring the benefits claimed, it might have been expected that their findings would have been published in a blaze of publicity - particularly in the run-up to the election, when there were signs that this highly controversial policy could have become a significant issue.

It is difficult to avoid the conclusion that perhaps HMI has not found that opting out has had an effect on standards; at least, not opting out in the sense of simply the change in management and organisation within schools. It would be surprising if the additional resources enjoyed by GM schools did not have quite a marked effect on standards; surprising, too, if the raising of morale that is widely claimed as a benefit of opting out did not also have an uplifting effect - but that, too, is likely to be linked to the additional resources. The fact is, of course, that such a message would be most unwelcome to the Government, which is committed to reducing expenditure on public services such as education, and certainly not one to which it would wish to draw attention. Since any HMI report which made such observations would inevitably attract great attention, this may be the reason that none has been published.

The only comment from HMI on GM schools so far, the first part of which ministers have been pleased to quote, is that 'Standards of work in grant-maintained schools were rather higher than those in the maintained sector as a whole and many of the schools had been able to improve the quality and extent of their accommodation, equipment, book stock and other learning resources through the use of capital grants and a redeployment of recurrent grant now within their control'.[4] Not only is reference made to favourable resources, but it is necessary to set this observation in the context that, amongst the GM schools visited, there was a substantial proportion of grammar schools and others with a predominantly middle-class and relatively advantaged intake; it would have been strange had HMI found anything else in the circumstances. There is, anyway, no suggestion that there has been any *improvement* in standards in GM schools.

The extent to which so many parents, despite this lack of evidence, have been prepared to go along with opting out - almost as an act of faith - is not as strange as it may appear. For some it *is* an act of faith, in a Government in which they believe; it is often such individuals who are responsible for raising the issue in schools - and the Conservative Party works actively and hard through its constituency associations to encourage members and supporters, especially those that are parents, teachers or school governors, to do exactly that.

For others, opting out has presented an opportunity to express their faith in a school that was threatened with closure, or some other form of re-organisation of which they disapproved; in other words to express faith in the *status quo*.

For many, it has offered the opportunity, even if it turns out to be only short-term, to increase the level of resources in their school - from which their own children will benefit. Often in such cases, as we have seen, it is headteachers that are central in promoting the concept - and some have shamelessly made the issue appear one of faith in their own judgement and professional abilities.

Opting out is a complex issue. In many respects all is not what it would seem, and this offers scope for a wide variety of interpretations and opinions. Its origins as a policy may be relatively clear - if not widely appreciated - but it appears to have taken on a life of its own. It is something of a Frankenstein's monster, beyond the control of even its creators. It has changed direction and seems not to be performing the function for which it was originally created. Or is it? Two possible interpretations of what has happened offer somewhat different answers to this question.

First, the policy may have been conceived by unabashed free-marketeers with the ear of the Government, with the intention of simply injecting an element of competition into the system. Opting out would act as a catalyst for change that would result in standards rising as LEAs were made more responsive to the demands of parents armed with the ultimate sanction of removing their school from the authority. This would be particularly likely in left-wing LEAs where, the Government believed, much educational policy was out of line with general public opinion and aspirations. In the event, parents elsewhere - particularly in low-spending Conservative-controlled shire authorities - seized the opportunity intended primarily for their inner-city counterparts. The rhetoric of criticism of LEAs was back-firing, and thus a different rationale was hastily created and promoted. Opting out became an opportunity for all, tied increasingly to the rhetoric of choice and parent power.

Alternatively, a more cynical interpretation is possible, in which the present situation - that opting out could be extended so widely as to replace the existing system - was not only a clear possibility, predicted by many at the time, but was always the intention. Promoting such a radical objective openly might have been foolhardy. Instead, a far more gentle line was judged to be politically expedient. There can be no doubt that such a discussion took place at the highest level of government, and resulted in a highly publicised difference of opinion between the then Prime Minister and her Secretary of State for Education. As the TES subsequently reported:

> Conservative councillors left a meeting this week with Mr Kenneth Baker, the Education Secretary, reassured that there would be no wholesale 'opting out' of schools from local authority control - despite an earlier assertion to the contrary by the Prime Minister.

> Mrs Thatcher had said that opting out was potentially 'as big as the one million transfer from the public sector (in housing) into owner-occupation' - and that she expected most schools would leave LEA control.
>
> But Mr Paul White, leader of the Conservative group on the Association of County Councils ... said the Education Secretary had insisted that few schools would opt out.
>
> Mr White said: 'We were very concerned at the Prime Minister's astonishing statement but we are much happier having spoken to Mr Baker.' [5]

The question is whether the difference of opinion was over the policy itself, or its public presentation. Whatever the truth of that (and it may never be known), it is clear that if even Conservative politicians found the idea of widespread opting out astonishing, it would have met with enormous resistance from the electorate in general. The fact that it was plainly Mrs Thatcher's intention that most schools would opt out adds weight to the suggestion that the softened line was essentially presentational. There are not many examples of Mrs Thatcher changing her mind, but it is quite likely that she was persuaded that only a more subtle approach would deliver the result she - and the free-marketeers - wished.

If this seems far-fetched to the average reader, it certainly will not to those with experience of the political process. It is a cliché - but a true one - to describe politics as 'the art of the possible'; successful politicians not only know what they want, they know how to get it - and will often resort to quite cynical lengths to achieve their ends. By a clever approach, the impossible can be made possible. It is only five years since it seemed impossible that most schools would opt out, yet it is now an objective that its advocates claim is within their reach. In the choice between the 'cock-up' and 'conspiracy' theories that are the alternative explanations for how this has come about, it is worth a brief look at the evidence of a clever conspiracy; the creation of a policy that can be made attractive for one purpose (or several) whilst actually serving another; a product that can be marketed under a label which obscures the true manufacturer.

Opting out can be - and has been - made to appeal to different groups for different reasons. Despite ministerial assurances to the contrary, it has been a lifeboat for schools facing closure. Despite assurances that GM schools would be funded at the same level as they would if they remained within LEAs, they have always been funded at a higher level. Despite assurances that they would not be able to change their character, they have been able to subtly introduce changes of admissions policy - and now, anyway, are free to apply at any time for a formal change of character. Through this variety of appeal, it was not hard to attract a number of 'takers' - if not as many as intended.

As some schools in an area opt out (for whatever reason), the pressure on others to do the same grows in a variety of ways. The attendant 'hype' surrounding GM schools suggests that they will be more attractive to parents, thus threatening to 'poach' pupils (and therefore funds) from neighbouring schools - which then see opting out as the means to retain equal status. As more schools opt out, taking 'their share' of funds from the LEA, the authority is unable to maintain the same level of support and services for the remainder - which then see opting out as the means to retain equal funding. Thus the policy has its own, in-built momentum.

As opting out spreads, the inevitability of grant levels to GM schools being cut as the cost becomes excessive is offered as a reason for opting out quickly, whilst some financial advantage remains. Similarly, the growing likelihood that the spread of opting out will lead to a two-tier system becomes a reason for doing it quickly, in order to avoid being in the lower tier. Thus, even major arguments against the policy of opting out can be turned round and used as arguments for doing it soon. It is possible that this may have come about by chance, but it is surely more likely - and more consistent with events themselves - that it is the result of careful planning.

Another key feature of the policy is that the progress of opting out has been determined school by school, as the decision rests with the parents of current pupils in the school concerned. Even if, therefore, the opting out of a particular school is demonstrably against the interests of pupils in other schools, or even perhaps not in the longer-term interests of the school itself, many of those actually taking the decision are likely to be motivated primarily by the narrow, or short-term, consequences as they affect their own children. The future of the education service in several areas has thus already been largely shaped by the random decisions of parents in individual schools, acting (often) in an essentially selfish manner.

In a speech to the Adam Smith Institute, John Major appeared to suggest that steps might be taken to ensure that measures such as opting out spread *even if people do not choose them*:

> In the 1980s we opened doors ... People with enterprise flocked through those doors with enthusiasm. But others felt that opportunities were not for them ... In the 1990s we mean to widen the avenue to choice and freedom. We mean to empower not just the enterprising, but all people - the least well-off - those most dependent on public services as well.[6]

Such a suggestion is consistent with views earlier expressed by the previous Education Secretary, Kenneth Clarke, who was reportedly 'enthusiastic for opting out, but would like to see the procedure simplified without parental ballots ... He would like to see decisions on opting out taken on the basis of the viability of the school, a firm business plan and continued strong leadership from the head and senior staff'.[7] Such a model would be more in line with the opt out procedures in the health service. Bob Balchin, chair of the GMS Foundation, said,

> 'We must look at ways in which balloting could be made easier

but also at ways of dispensing with ballots in certain cases. If there is not much aggro in senior management and governing bodies why bother with the ballot? I've never believed that we have ever been talking about GMS giving power to parents. It is giving authority to the governing body to make policy, and the professional staff to run the school well'.[8]

The White Paper does indeed include a proposal which would enable some schools (those judged to be failing their pupils) to be made grant-maintained without a parental ballot, after first being removed by the Secretary of State from the control of their governing bodies and LEAs and put under the stewardship of an Education Association.

The publication of the White Paper, and the subsequent Bill, will inevitably lead to a major public debate on the best way forward for the school system as a whole. As the statistics at the start of this chapter show, opting out has yet to penetrate far into that system - although vigorous attempts have been made to create the opposite impression. In the next chapter we shall look at the main aspects of the White Paper, and the implications for the school service of its proposals, before moving on in the final chapter to consider the importance of that public debate in determining the way forward.

NOTES

1   The Carlton Club Political Committee, *Education in the 1990s*, 1991.

2   *The Role and Function of Governing Bodies of Grant-Maintained Schools*, DES, March 1992.

3   *Hansard*, 3.2.92.

4   *Education in England 1990-91*, The Annual Report of HM Senior Chief Inspector of Schools.

5   *TES*, 18.9.87.

6   *The Next Phase of Conservatism: the Privatisation of Choice*, speech by John Major, 16.6.92.

7   *Education*, 23.11.90.

8   *Managing Schools Today*, Vol 1 No 1, 1991.

10

THE WHITE PAPER

The White Paper, *Choice and Diversity - A New Framework for schools* was published on 28 July 1992.[1] It had been preceded by an extraordinary level of 'hype', ever since the Secretary of State announced his plans not only to publish it, but to write key parts of it himself. He billed it then as 'the last piece of the jigsaw to bring the organisational framework together, taking account of the grant-maintained revolution. It will provide a clear statement of how we expect education to be over the next twenty-five years,'[2] and described it at the press launch as 'radical, sensible and in tune with what parents want'.[3] Whether or not it is in tune with what parents want will become apparent over the coming year or two, and will determine the future of the school service for very much longer than that.

Responses were required by 25 September, a very similar consultation period to that for the 1988 Act - just when schools, and many of those concerned with them, are on holiday and cannot easily communicate with each other. The main proposals were as follows:

> A new body, the Funding Agency for Schools, will be responsible for the payment of grant to GM schools. Also, the Agency will share responsibility with LEAs for planning the provision of school places. It will start to share this responsibility once ten per cent of either primary or secondary pupils in the LEA concerned are in GM schools (the 10 per cent entry point); once 75 per cent of either are in GM schools, the Agency will take over sole responsibility for this function. The present requirement for LEAs to have an education committee will be removed.

LEAs and the Funding Agency will be required to review and report annually to the Secretary of State on the supply of places in their respective sectors. The Secretary of State will have new powers to direct either or both to bring forward rationalisation proposals and to bring forward proposals of his own, in which case he must arrange a public inquiry.

A Common Funding Formula for GM schools will be introduced, LEA by LEA, as the number of schools opting out justifies it, from April 1994. It will be based on the Government's Standard Spending Assessment for the LEA concerned.

The present requirement for LEAs to delegate at least 85 per cent of their potential schools budget by April 1993 will be increased beyond that date, with further simplification of LMS formulae and encouragement to move to 'maximum delegation' and service level agreements (described in Chapter 8).

Legislation will allow LEAs (subject to designation by the Secretary of State) to provide services to GM schools even when this means employing more staff than required for its own needs, but for a maximum of two years.

GM schools and LEAs will be encouraged to co-operate on admissions. The Secretary of State will have the power to impose common procedures and LEAs will have the power to direct any LEA or GM school to admit a pupil who has no school place.

The transition of schools to GM status (ie. opting out) will be eased: the present requirement for a second governors' resolution before a parental ballot can be held will be dropped; LEA expenditure on publishing information for parents about a ballot will be limited, and governors will be given a grant to the same limit;

the minimum size of a GM primary school governing body will be reduced from 15 to 11 (three parent governors, one teacher, the head and six first or foundation governors); small primary schools will be able to propose opting out as a cluster; GM schools will be given power to provide part-time as well as full-time nursery education.

Any maintained school (LEA or GM) which is named in a statement of Special Educational Need will be required to admit the child concerned. The LEA and Funding Agency, from the 10 per cent entry point, will share the duty to ensure sufficient places for pupils with statements. The Secretary of State will have powers to require the rationalisation of special schools, which will be enabled to apply for GM status.

Diversity and specialisation, particularly in technology, will be encouraged. A new category of 'Sponsor Governor' will be created. The Technology Schools Initiative will be extended, and the creation of new Technology Colleges will be encouraged in partnership with business sponsors. LEA and GM schools will be able to apply to become GM Technology Colleges, but LEA schools will be required to go through the normal opt out ballot procedure before publishing their proposals for GMTC status.

Inspection reports will identify schools 'at risk' of failing to provide an acceptable education. The governing body of such a school will be required to produce an action plan, with a supporting commentary from the LEA - which will have new powers to appoint additional governors or withdraw delegation from 'at risk' schools.

The Secretary of State will have new powers to replace any or all of the first governors of a GM school at risk (or in other circumstances where he is satisfied that their actions prejudice the effective provision of education).

The Secretary of State will have power to appoint Education Associations to take over the management of 'at risk' schools - singly or in groups - from their governing bodies and LEAs. An Education Association will have the powers and funding of a GM governing body; it will be given limited time to bring schools up to a satisfactory standard. If successful, the schools will become grant-maintained (without a ballot); Education Associations will also have the power to propose closure of schools. Voluntary aided (mostly church) schools will not be subject to this intervention, but the Government is consulting the Churches on the need for additional powers.

The National Curriculum Council and the School Examination and Assessment Council will be replaced by a new School Curriculum and Assessment Authority (which is not within the remit of this book to consider).

Perhaps the most striking feature of the White Paper is the number of new powers proposed for the Secretary of State, which provoked *The Times* leader (29 July 1992) to comment: 'The government is dismayed at Britain's poor education record and has responded as governments always respond. It has blamed everybody but itself, and decided to nationalise the schools'.

Much of the reaction to the White Paper, like most of the speculation before it, centred on the extension of opting out and the possible demise of LEAs; in both instances, there were dramatic claims from some of the press that thousands, most and even all schools would opt out. This may be the government's wish, but even the White Paper claims only that 'on a simple projection of current trends, there *could* be over 1,500 GM schools by April 1994' and that 'by 1996 most of the 3,900 maintained secondary schools, as well a significant proportion of the 19,000 [*sic*] maintained primary schools, *could* be grant maintained' (author's emphasis) - figures described by the *Independent* (29 July) as 'merely a statistical guesstimate'.

The headteacher associations were sceptical. A spokesman for the National Association of Head Teachers said, 'All the government's estimates to date in every possible area have never reached their target', and complained that 'In recent years too many of the reforms in the school system have been driven by dogma, politics and confrontation, rather than the need to ensure that every child in this country benefits from the highest standard of education possible'.[4] The spokesman for the Secondary Heads Association predicted that most schools would react cautiously, 'particularly if the future looks like a lot of empty promises. Most of our members will respond in a pragmatic way to reality rather than be guided by political principle'. He added that 'there is no strong evidence that the paper is in tune with what parents want'.[5]

The key question is, what will parents make of the proposals? The answer may lie in the extent to which they allow themselves to be guided by rhetoric, rather than examining the proposals themselves and assessing the implications. We shall therefore put aside any assumption that thousands of schools will opt out just because it is said that they will, and look at the White Paper's proposals to see if they are really likely to encourage such a change.

The Funding Agency for Schools, when set up, would be a statutory national body with 10-15 members appointed by the Secretary of State; 'A substantial number of the members will come from outside education, including key appointments from the industrial and commercial worlds', 'The Funding Agency will acquire functions as and when the number of GM schools increases and the Secretary of State so determines' and it would be able to set up regional offices as required, subject to approval from the Secretary of State. Its initial role would be to take over from the

Department for Education the payment of grant to, and financial monitoring of, GM schools. Once ten per cent of either primary or secondary pupils in an LEA area are in GM schools, it would then share responsibility with the authority both for the rationalisation of school places and for securing sufficient places. Once 75 per cent of either primary or secondary pupils are in GM schools, the Agency would take sole responsibility for these matters; LEAs could apply to be relieved of their duty to secure sufficient places before that point. Both bodies would be required to report annually on the supply of places in their sector to the Secretary of State, who would be able to direct either or both to produce rationalisation plans. The Secretary of State would also be able to put forward proposals of his own, but this would require him to arrange a public inquiry - for which he appoints the Inspector to make recommendations on his, and the other, proposals before taking the final decision himself.

In practice, it could take a long time in many areas for the proportion of pupils in GM schools in the secondary (or, theoretically, primary) sector to increase from the very low threshold of ten per cent to the rather high ceiling of 75 per cent. During this period, responsibility for school provision (opening, closing and amalgamating schools) would be shared by the elected local authority and the appointed Funding Agency (and, possibly, an Education Association), each of which may have different priorities, and each of which would be responsible for schools funded according to different formulae and criteria. If this arrangement failed to produce an outcome to the liking of the Secretary of State, he could intervene with his own plans - subject only to having to consider (not accept or follow) the recommendations of a public inquiry for which he appointed the Inspector. There is great emphasis in the paper (obviously encouraged by the Treasury) on the removal of surplus school capacity, which implies that the

170

government will be less inclined in future to frustrate LEA plans by allowing schools to opt out to escape reorganisation.

Between the ten per cent threshold and 75 per cent ceiling, voluntary bodies would be able to propose the opening of new schools either with voluntary aided or GM status (opening a new school, in this sense, would include obtaining VA or GM status for an existing independent school). In either case the final decision is for the Secretary of State, and plainly would be influenced by the overall position on the supply of school places in the area. However, the White Paper does appear to open the door (but how far is not clear) to applications for denominational schools from religious voluntary bodies such as Muslims, Seventh-Day Adventists and Evangelical Christians - all of whom have been pressing for such opportunities. It may also enable some 'public' schools, to become funded as part of the state system.

The Common Funding Formula for calculating the annual maintenance grant of GM schools would be introduced LEA by LEA ('when there are sufficient schools to justify it') from April 1994 and would be based on the government's Standard Spending Assessment. 'The CFF will secure that over time schools across the country will be funded on a consistent basis derived from the Government's own view of the appropriate level of spending in an area.' In other words, the government would gradually gain *direct* control over school spending. As we saw in Chapter 2, it already has considerable indirect control, but LEAs are still free to adjust budgets according to their own local priorities, and most currently spend above SSA level on education (we shall return to this point later). Incidentally, the term Common Funding Formula is somewhat misleading, as it implies that the formula would be common to all GM schools. Whilst many GM schools (notably those that had opted out of low spending LEAs) were pressing for a national formula, the CFF will be common only to GM schools within the same LEA area. The government will be consulting further on the details of funding arrangements.

The White Paper clearly signals the reduction of some specific grants to GM schools: 'These grants will be kept under review. The expectation is that, as schools gain more experience of local management of schools, they will need less financial help in the transition to GM status. The Government will continue to make available on a yearly rolling programme funds for the capital development of GM schools. Totals will be decided annually as part of the Public Expenditure Survey.' This is further evidence of the role of the Treasury, which is intent on further reducing public expenditure over the next few years.

The proposal to require LEAs to reach levels of budget delegation greater than 85 per cent, and to encourage 'maximum delegation', would have the effect of further reducing, and perhaps eliminating, any significant differences in either the funding level or management autonomy between the LEA and GM sectors. As we have seen, many LEAs are moving rapidly in this direction ahead of the statutory timetable. Ultimately, the main issue to be decided, and this is an issue to which I shall return, may be whether the few strategic decisions that remain in a system of largely autonomous schools are best entrusted to a government appointed body or a locally elected one.

The White Paper makes clear that LEAs are not currently permitted to provide services to GM schools if this involves them employing staff in addition to those required for their own needs; LEAs may now only trade at the margin of capacity. 'The Government expects that increasingly the private sector will step in to provide such services' but LEAs would be given additional powers to enable them to fill the gap (for a maximum of two years) until the private sector is in a position to do so. Most schools have been unaware that opting out would lead to the virtually automatic privatisation of services, and it is doubtful that private companies will find it profitable to offer a complete range of the services that schools use. It is also doubtful that LEAs will be able to manage effectively, or recruit staff for, such temporary arrangements. It seems probable that a few LEAs, with a significant proportion of GM schools buying back their services, are already trading in an unlawful manner.

The paper also recognises other difficulties that have arisen in the few areas where there is a concentration of GM schools, and proposes the removal of some of their autonomy over admissions and exclusions. GM schools and LEAs are to be encouraged to co-operate over admissions, but the Secretary of State would have the power to impose a common procedure. In addition, LEAs would be able to direct any LEA or GM school to admit a pupil without a school place (subject to appeal to the Secretary of State in the case of GM schools). Coupled with the proposed requirement to admit any child with a statement of special educational needs which names the school, and the Secretary of State's new power to replace any or all of a GM school's first governors, the White Paper in fact represents a significant potential erosion of the present autonomy of the GM sector.

The measures proposed to 'ease the transition of schools to GM status' (ie. to speed-up opting out) would mean that parents would receive up to six weeks less notice of a ballot on opting out (which would follow a single governors' resolution) and that LEAs would be restricted to a single mailing of information to parents, the cost of which would be limited 'to the equivalent of one leaflet'. Governing bodies would receive a grant to match the expenditure limit on the LEA, but the paper does not say whether they would also have to stick to that limit or whether, as now, they could also use (LEA derived) school funds to promote opting out. There is a reminder that LEAs are obliged to be 'objective, balanced, informative and

173

accurate' but, again, nothing is said about a similar obligation on governing bodies.

The proposed arrangements for small primary schools to opt out in clusters demonstrate a remarkable faith in the willingness of participants to co-operate in an otherwise highly competitive environment. Prospective cluster schools would hold separate ballots on cluster GM status. If some reject the idea, the others could choose whether or not to proceed without them. If approved, a cluster would be managed by a single governing body similar to that of a conventional GM school (thus reversing the general requirement of the 1980 Act that not more than two primary schools should share a common governing body). Five parent governors and two teacher governors would be elected by an electoral college of all the schools; a headteacher governor would be chosen each year by the group of heads. The governing body would be responsible for the budget of the cluster, but 'the Government intends that cluster schools should be subject to the same market discipline as other schools'. Parents, therefore, would continue to apply to individual schools, not the cluster, for admission, and the governing body would be required 'to ensure that the majority of funds follow the pupil'. After delegating an amount of the grant to each school to cover their basic running costs, the governing body would 'be free to deploy the remaining funds as it sees fit, for the benefit of the cluster as a whole'. Staff who transfer to the cluster would be employed by the governing body, which would also have the power to publish statutory proposals to enlarge significantly, change the character of, or close any of the schools in the cluster.

Under such arrangements, the larger members of the cluster would be in a position, through their greater voting power in the parent and teacher governor elections, to achieve greater representation on the governing body. This would enable them, through the control of the budget, staffing and maybe even the publication of statutory proposals, to secure their own priorities - possibly at the expense of their smaller, and more vulnerable, partners. All of this, of course, would happen only some time after the decision had been taken about whether or not to opt out as part of a cluster (and regardless of any assurances given at that time).

The proposal to give GM schools the power to provide part-time, as well as full-time, nursery education is an acknowledgement that - as pointed out by Local Schools Information in late 1990 - due to an anomaly in present law they do not have such power other than when acting as agents of the LEA. In lengthy correspondence with LSI, the Department for Education strongly disputed this view at the time, as reported in the *TES* of 1 February 1991. Now, however, the White Paper says that 'The Government will legislate to remove this anomaly'.

If the encouragement of specialisation in schools is to lead to greater parental choice over the education of their children, it is bound to lead to a much greater increase in the selection of pupils than is acknowledged in the White Paper. The issue of selection is politically highly sensitive, as we have already seen. Possibly for this reason, there has been an apparently deliberate switch of emphasis from selection to specialisation as the means for introducing diversity. This point, too, is one that requires further attention, and to which we shall return.

The proposals for 'Sponsor Governors' and Technology Colleges modelled on CTCs (but dropping the requirement for an urban, 'City', location) display the triumph of optimism over experience in respect of the enthusiasm of industry and commerce to invest directly in schools. The CTC programme is still five short of its original, modest target of twenty, and the government has had to resort to the injection of far more public money than it had planned to bring even these to fruition. Most of the large, prestigious companies that do take an active interest in educational developments have preferred, so far, to do so in partnership with LEAs, rather than align themselves behind ventures that are plainly intended to undermine the role of local authorities in the education service.

Finally, before returning to the three key issues of funding, democratic control and specialisation/selection, let us look at the White Paper's proposals for schools 'at risk' and the introduction of Education Associations to sort them out.

The intention is that the new, independent (privatised) teams of school inspectors, hired by governing bodies to report on their schools, will identify those schools 'at risk' of failing to give their pupils an acceptable education. In addition, the Secretary of State will be able to ask HM Chief Inspector to inspect 'any school about which he receives particularly disturbing reports'. The paper makes clear that 'The onus for improving schools rests in the first instance on governing bodies and their head teachers', but LEAs would be given back-up powers to appoint additional governors and to withdraw delegation, giving the authority control of staffing (subject to the governors' right of appeal to the Secretary of State). It should be remembered that it was the 1988 Act, and LMS, that removed from LEAs the powers that it is now proposed should be restored to them - although they will still not be able to deploy additional financial resources to support a failing school. If the Secretary of State were satisfied that the governing body and/or LEA were proposing an effective course of action, he would allow them up to a year to improve the school; if, during or at the end of that year, 'it became plain that the plan was not working', he could place the school under the management of an Education Association - which he could also do from the outset if he thought that the plan put forward would not work.

An Education Association would, in effect, 'be in the

position of a GM governing body but appointed by the Secretary of State'. It would consist of a chairman and 'typically some five other part-time members' (such as, apparently, retired headteachers), and would be set up 'when the first candidate for EA stewardship emerged within a particular area'. It could subsequently take in as many schools in the area, including neighbouring LEAs, as were found to be failing'. The EAs would receive grant for maintaining its school(s) from the Secretary of State on the same basis as for GM schools and, where it controlled more than one school, it would determine the allocation of funds amongst them. It would also have access to the other grants available to GM schools, with 'discretion to determine their allocation across the schools'. An EA would be set a remit, and timescale, by the Secretary of State; its task in a school 'may require staffing changes at the senior management level and within its teaching force'. If successful, 'the normal expectation is that the school will then become grant-maintained' (without a ballot); the EA would also have the power to propose closure of a school.

The principle that schools should not be allowed to persistently fail their pupils is entirely laudable; the Inner London Education Authority (in its final years, before it was abolished by the 1988 Act) pioneered a system for dealing with schools 'at risk' (it even used the same term) upon which the White Paper's scheme is plainly modelled. But the mechanism proposed for resolving the problem through Education Associations is, at best, unnecessarily centralist and, possibly, extremely sinister. It could represent the Government's answer on how to make schools grant-maintained even when parents have no wish to opt out - or, as John Major expressed it (see page 163), 'to empower not just the enterprising, but all people'.

It could be that no more than a handful of schools, which most people would agree to be failing their pupils, and of which the governing bodies and even the LEAs had been unable (for whatever reason) to turn around, would be handed over to Education Associations to sort out or close. However, the powers proposed would enable something far more radical. An EA or, indeed, several EAs - hand-picked by the Secretary of State - could be put in charge of a large number of schools, provided that the Secretary of State had been prompted by 'disturbing reports' (from whom?) to obtain a view from HM Chief Inspector (who is appointed by the Secretary of State) that they were 'at risk', and that he had satisfied himself that their governing bodies' and LEAs' plans had not effected, or were not likely to effect, an adequate improvement. An EA would have far more power than an LEA, having control of the (GM) budgets of all of its schools *with the freedom to switch funds between schools, to hire and fire staff and to propose the closure of schools* before returning the successful ones to (presumably new) governing bodies as GM schools. This hypothesis may seem an unduly cynical response to the proposals but, if such powers would not be used, for what purpose are they being sought?

Let us now look in more detail at the three issues which lie at the heart of the White Paper or, at least, at the heart of its relevance to the extension of opting out: funding, democratic control and diversity/specialisation - and its link with selection. Of these, the first and last are addressed specifically, if not very openly, in the paper; institutional accountability, rather than democratic control, is a theme of the paper but, as we have considered elsewhere, this is a poor substitute.

Within days of the publication of the White Paper, there were already problems for the government over its proposals for funding GM schools through a formula linked to Standard Spending Assessments. The majority of LEAs spend more than their SSA on education; only a handful spend significantly below it. Thus, a move to funding at SSA would lead to cuts in spending in schools which opted out of most LEAs. Under the headline 'Funding blow to opt out schools', the *Guardian* (1 August 1992) reported that:

> Thousands of schools would have no financial incentive to opt out of local authority control under this week's education white paper because the proposed funding formula would leave them less money. But amendments are already being made to the published plan aimed at persuading nearly all 4,000 secondary schools in England to opt out in four years ... Stephen Byers, the Labour MP for Wallsend, pointed out this 'flaw at the heart of the white paper'. A spokeswoman [for the Department for Education] said that an opt out school could apply to be exempt from the new formula although the alternative had not yet been worked out. Mr Byers said there was now panic at the Department. 'John Patten declared the white paper would lay the foundation for the next 25 years yet, within 72 hours, key sections of the document are being rewritten.'

The *Sunday Times* (9 August 1992) carried a similar story under the very prominent headline 'Opt out schools could be target of spending cuts', which included several quotes from anxious GM headteachers. Almost as if designed to strengthen Mr Patten's position in his negotiations with the Treasury, the article said:

> An education department spokesman acknowledged there could be reductions in funding in over-spending authorities, but emphasised that schools would have a right of appeal to the secretary of state. 'It's beyond belief that the government would let its flagship flounder on something like this. Any suggestion of winners or losers is way off the mark' said another (anonymous) source. The new formula, which will be spelt out in detail in a consultation paper later this year, will be introduced area by area from 1994. By that time, officials believe, the threat of capping and restraints on public spending will have forced councils to bring their budgets into line with government estimates.

Incidentally, a move to funding GM schools at SSA level would put the few authorities which spend well below it under irresistable pressure to increase education spending up to that level. For them, this would require either cuts in other services - and, in practice, that would mean social services, as housing budgets are 'ring-fenced' (ie. cannot be used for other purposes) and others are too small to make any significant contribution - or an increase in Council Tax, and possible capping.

There is also a further, more technical, aspect to the issue of SSAs that could still lead to cuts for GM schools. Each council (as we saw in Chapter 2) is given an education SSA, which is the level of spending that the government believes to be appropriate for that area. However, the overall education figure is made up of five sub-blocks covering different types of provision: primary, secondary, under-5, post-16 and 'other' (which includes adult education). Even if councils are forced to cut their budgets back to the government's figures, they are free to decide how spending should be allocated within the total - regardless of the government's assessment of the sub-blocks. Thus, many councils spend less than their SSA sum on under-5 and adult education and put the money, instead, into school provision. A move to funding at SSA level for schools would thus have the effect of removing this subsidy. A simple example, based on very similar figures to those for an actual authority (assuming that all of its secondary schools are 11-16), illustrates the possible consequences:

	Education SSA	Actual expenditure
Primary	£62.0 million	£64.0 million
Secondary	70.0	72.5
Under-5	7.0	5.0
Post-16	35.0	34.0
Other	8.0	6.5
Total	£182.0 million	£182.0 million

Thus a move to funding the schools at SSA level would remove £2.5 million (almost 3.5 per cent) from the secondary schools and £2 million from the primary schools.

It is not at all clear how the Government will attempt to

resolve these problems, but two things are obvious: all schools are likely to feel the government squeeze on council spending in the next few years; and opting out could become a classic case of jumping out of the frying pan into the fire.

The discretion that councils have to make decisions on spending that they believe are right for their local communities raises the issue of democratic control. Under the White Paper's proposals, it is not only the funding of schools that would come under the control of central government, rather than local authorities. Planning of school provision, the closing and (perhaps) opening of schools, would increasingly be in the hands of a government-appointed body and the Secretary of State. So, too, would school admissions, the provision of special education, the creation of new types of school and the fate of schools with problems. This would certainly amount to the end of the school service as 'a national system, *locally administered*' (see page 21). It is to be hoped that, whatever the imperfections of local government, the proposition that such a major service should be removed from local democratic influence will provoke, at least, a vigorous debate and that the possible consequences of such a move are considered fully before irrevocable decisions are made.

The last major issue, that of specialisation and selection, is, like funding, one that will have significant practical implications for very many children - and their parents. The Government's declared aim is to increase parental choice of school by increasing the diversity amongst schools, but there is an inevitable link between choice, diversity and selection which is not properly acknowledged in the White Paper.

Parental choice is not increased by diversity unless there is a realistic prospect of gaining admission to schools that are not necessarily the closest, yet proximity is normally the

major factor in schools' admissions policies - apart from
selective schools. A parent with a musical child, living
near a school which specialises in technology, or modern
languages, will gain nothing from diversity if the school
which specialises in music is on the other side of town - and
will be filled by pupils with a stronger case under its
(non-selective) admissions policy. Only if such schools
give some priority to children with a particular ability or
aptitude, regardless of where they live, will diversity lead to
choice.

Yet, to give priority to such children requires selection -
by some means - of those children from amongst the many
who may apply. (There would be no such problem in
schools which were under-subscribed, but there will be far
fewer of these as surplus places are removed through the
programme of rationalisation envisaged in the White Paper.)
A significant change of character in a school requires a
formal, statutory procedure to be followed under the 1980
Education Act (Sections 12 and 13), and such a change of
character includes 'in particular ... the making or alteration
of arrangements for the admission of pupils by reference to
ability *or aptitude*' (Sec.16(2) - author's emphasis).

A Department for Education circular (11/88) on
admission of pupils says:

> For schools whose admission arrangements are based on
> selection by reference to ability or aptitude, it will need to be
> made clear how the selection procedure operates. Non-selective
> schools may not have as criteria for admission any arrangements
> which involve selection by reference to ability or aptitude. *This
> includes any arro gements which, by implication, carry an
> element of selection, such as headteacher interview to assess the
> qualities that the applicants might bring to the school* (author's
> emphasis).

The White Paper's first chapter, 'Schools into a new century',
says:

> A school that wishes to develop its strengths and place an

emphasis on particular teaching skills can usually do so within its existing powers. It generally does not constitute a significant change of character requiring the approval of the Secretary of State ... The fact that a school is strong in a particular field may increase the demand to attend, but it does not necessarily follow that selective entry criteria have to be imposed by the school. The selection that takes place is parent-driven. The principle of open access remains ... For a non-selective school to become selective - or vice versa - involves a significant change of character ... It is not the Government's intention either to encourage or to discourage such applications.

Shortly before the White Paper was published, the Secretary of State, John Patten, wrote an article entitled 'Who's afraid of the 'S' word?', in which he said:

Selection is not, and should not be, a great issue of the 1990s as it was in the 1960s. The S-word for socialists to come to terms with is, rather, "specialisation". The fact is that children excel at different things; it is foolish to ignore it, and some schools may wish specifically to cater for these differences. Specialisation, underpinned by the National Curriculum, will be the answer for some - though not all - children, driven by aptitude and interest as much as ability.[6]

So, in both the White Paper and his article, Mr Patten has not only played down the link between specialisation and selection, he has actually implied that one will supplant the other - apparently ignoring the fact that the legal position over the character of a school and selection applies as much to aptitude as it does to ability. The selection that takes place can only be parent-driven up the capacity of the school; if the demand to attend exceeds that capacity, there must then be some criteria for deciding which children to admit. These can only be based on proximity (thus making parental choice a hollow promise) or on the qualities that the child might bring to the school (thus involving a significant change of character).

Contrary to Mr Patten's assertion, there is therefore every prospect that selection *will* become a great issue of the 1990s if his proposals are implemented. The fact that it could be selection by aptitude, rather than by ability, will merely add to the controversy, for aptitude (let alone interest) in a child of eleven is surely impossible to assess objectively - and therefore fairly. Over-subscribed, specialist schools would increasingly be in a position to choose their pupils, rather than be chosen by parents, but the criteria would be far less clear. The number of aggrieved parents, particularly if their expectations had been even further raised by all the rhetoric of increased choice, would be likely to soar.

The Government will doubtless seek to reassure parents by pointing out that popular schools will be enabled to expand in response to demand, but that will not happen overnight. Producing more of the particular kind of education that parents decide they want is not just a matter of stepping up the output of the relevant production line. However much the advocates of market forces may wish, or pretend, that education is simply a commodity that can be traded like any other ('be it vegetables or motor cars'- see page 52), they are wrong. It is a public service, which should be available to all on more or less equal terms, and which is far more complex in its provision than has recently been acknowledged by the often simplistic approach of the reforms that have been proposed to remedy its undoubted deficiencies.

The way forward is neither as smooth, nor as straight, as the path suggested by the White Paper; already significant potholes have been found, and there will doubtless be more. In the final chapter, we shall look a little more closely at the future for schools.

NOTES

1   *Choice and Diversity - A New Framework for Schools,*
    HMSO 1992.
2   *Guardian*, 19.5.92.
3   *The Times*, 29.7.92.
4   *TES*, 31.7.92.
5   *Education*, 31.7.92.
6   *New Statesman*, 17.7.92.

11
THE WAY FORWARD

There is a well-known joke in which a traveller asks the way to somewhere only to be told that he is starting from the wrong place. If any journey is to be completed successfully, it is essential not only to have the right directions but to know where you are setting out from - and it is often unwise to rely on a single opinion for either direction or starting point, let alone both, if the matter is in any doubt. Of course, the problem becomes insoluble if there is also doubt, or disagreement, over the destination!

In looking at our school system, there is more or less universal agreement over the need to improve the present position; to raise standards and levels of achievement. In his presidential address to the British Association in 1990, which attracted widespread publicity, Sir Claus Moser said:

> Britain is in danger of becoming one of the worst educated of all the industrial nations, with hundreds of thousands of children having education experiences not worthy of a civilised nation.

In response, Channel 4 Television established a Commission on Education 'to investigate the state of our education, and to recommend what might be done immediately to make improvements'.[1] The five members of the Commission (A.H.Halsey, Neville Postlethwaite, S.J.Prais, Alan Smithers and Hilary Steedman) brought a wide range of experience, a variety of political alignments and, above all, a very high level of professional qualification and authority. The Commission was widely welcomed, especially in the absence of a Royal Commission, which some observers regarded as the ideal mechanism for addressing the undeniable problems.

The Commission found that young people in Britain were not reaching the levels of achievement common elsewhere in Europe, and blamed the arrangements in both primary and secondary schools for this. It described English education as very good for its best pupils, and emphasised the importance of parental support, pre-school education and a high employment economy in motivating children and young people.[2] In a passage on legislative attempts to improve the system, the report said:

> The three tranches of reform - the 1944 Education Act, the Comprehensive Reforms of the 1970s, the Education Reform Act of 1988 - have all failed to provide Britain with an effective education system suitable for the technological world of today. The paradox of change without change is brought about because education is still heavily focused on the needs of the academic minority. The education system worked well for this group in 1900 and it still does so today. The needs of the majority in relation to their subsequent working life have been given far too little attention ...

The Commission also recognised the difficulties that lie ahead:

> Curing the problem will be much harder than diagnosing it. There have been so many changes in recent years that more will not be welcome. But changes must come. Our national future depends upon it. These changes must be based on empirical evidence not on ideology.

Most of the content of the report was concerned with what goes on within schools - the curriculum, examination system, and internal organisation. The recommendations covered the importance of English and basic arithmetic in primary schools; assessment, both diagnostic and external testing; progress being linked to attainment rather than just age, and the organisation of classes around similarity of attainment; specialisation for older children, with opportunities linked to career interests; a national curriculum differently structured from the present model;

the creation of three inter-connecting pathways at the upper secondary stage, with ample opportunity to switch between the academic, technical and vocational options; changes to the examination system; some re-allocation of resources from academic education to technical and vocational education; and improvement in the prospects for technically and vocationally qualified youngsters to move into skilled employment.

The Commission did not concern itself with the level of resourcing, nor with the structure and organisation of the school system in terms of the matters we are considering in this book - which many regard as a shame. However, another, uniquely qualified, observer did comment on these matters just before the publication of the White Paper.

Eric Bolton, former HM Senior Chief Inspector, in a speech to the Council of Local Education Authorities, emphasised the need to retain some degree of overall planning and organisation:

> Schools are becoming increasingly autonomous ... consequently, it is at school level that most of the important decisions about priorities for local spending will be made. No doubt many decisions will be sensible and intelligent. But they are self-interested decisions where the immediate concern is with what is of benefit to that particular institution. That will lead, and has already led, to some marked improvements in efficiency and value for money at the school level. However, it is surely the triumph of hope over experience to expect that such self interested, isolated, fragmented decisions ... will add up to a sensible and efficient national school system ...
>
> A national system of schooling, a proportion of which is compulsory, can be governed and administered in a variety of ways. It cannot, however, remain a public and equitable national service if it is to be shaped and determined by nothing other than the aggregation of the random, self-interested choices made by individuals in thousands of particular schools ... Without coherence and continuity, quality and standards of learning will not be raised.[3]

Echoing the findings of Channel 4's Commission, Mr Bolton said:

> English education's greatest success throughout history has been to fail most children. Our system is better than any other in the developed world at failing people, and turning them out with a sense that they have achieved nothing of value. It is the issue above all others that we need to address if we are to raise the standards of education.

The present concentration on opting out and the establishment of a market philosophy in schools is, at best, a damaging distraction from what should be the focus of attention. At worst, the consequences - the dependence of schools on a favourable 'market position', the importance of crude league tables in establishing that position, and the constant pressure on resources (of which the interest in opting out is both a direct and indirect manifestation) - will be to actually make the bad situation described by both the Commission and Eric Bolton *even worse*.

The contribution that academic pupils will make to the reputation - and league table position - of schools will tend to perpetuate the situation in which education is still heavily focused on their needs whilst the needs of the majority are given too little attention. Schools where there is a high proportion of children who lack the benefit of adequate support from parents, high-quality pre-schooling or good employment prospects to motivate them will find themselves being penalised financially as they are increasingly abandoned by the parents of other children who *are* able to exercise such a choice.

The Government is quite content to continue to introduce further change, despite the fact that, after so much in recent years, it is not widely welcome. However, unfortunately, it is apparently *not* willing to base change on empirical evidence, nor to listen to advice from those with great experience and no political axe to grind. Instead, it insists on the pursuit of its ideology.

189

Distraction or not from the matters of real importance, as things stand, it will be opting out which dominates the education headlines during the coming year or two, and doubtless a great many schools will consider whether they should or shouldn't opt out themselves. They will watch anxiously to see what others are doing. They will argue amongst themselves and with each other. Many of the issues we have raised in this book will be discussed - but money will probably dominate proceedings. Headteachers and governors will spend hours gathering information, calculating budgets, mustering arguments, preparing literature and so on. Others, who oppose their view (which may be for or against), will devote equal effort to achieving a different outcome.

Of course, this discussion will not take place in every school; not even in every secondary school. For the reasons that we have discussed, the creation and extension of an independent, grant-maintained sector as the 'sharp end' of an increasingly market-led system can come only as bad news for many schools - and for their pupils. It may be that, for some of them, an Education Association will take over responsibility from their governing bodies and LEAs. It will be interesting to see how long the Government's insistence will last that good education can be provided even in the most difficult circumstances with very few extra resources, once there is nobody left to blame but the government itself for the lack of such quality.

But overall, schools up and down the country will devote a fantastic amount of time and energy to an issue the outcome of which may do nothing to affect their educational standards. As Eric Bolton also observed (and he is better placed than most to know), 'What is not clear yet is whether or not there will be any feed-through from improved efficiency to higher standards and better quality. That is one of the many acts of faith embedded in the complex structure of the Education Reform Act'.

In the meantime, there will be little discussion (or at least a great deal less than there could, and should, be) of the vital issues of achievement and standards and the best way to raise them for all pupils.

So, what can be done to direct attention - and resources, both financial and human - towards the matters that should be demanding the most urgent consideration?

Most obviously, the opportunity presented when the issue of education is back in the public eye must be seized, as it was not during the last general election campaign, by all those concerned: heads, teachers, governors, local government politicians - even educationists! - and, above all, by parents. They must not allow themselves to be distracted by an item that is on the agenda, as we have sought to demonstrate, only because a handful of free-marketeers have successfully placed it there through their influence over government policy.

As we have seen, this is not a political issue where divisions occur simply along party lines. There are a great many Conservative supporters (and many Conservative politicians) who are strongly opposed to opting out; there are also Labour and Liberal-Democrat supporters (though not, perhaps, very many) who, whether or not they oppose the idea in principle, have gone along with it in practice. Concern to address the problems of low standards, inadequate achievement, and levels of expectation that do insufficient justice to the potential talents of children and young people (most damaging when they become inadequate levels of self-expectation) transcends party boundaries.

Only if the ideology (which many would describe as dogma) that has dominated the discussion of education policy in recent years is thrown out and replaced by an examination of the needs of young people, as well as the needs of the nation and those of industry and commerce, will any real progress be likely. Whilst it may not have been perfect, the 1944 Act achieved a degree of reform that generally brought enormous benefit to a large proportion of the population. It is no coincidence that it was the product of a carefully constructed social and political consensus.

In its conclusion, the Channel 4 Commission says that the transformation of our education system for which they argue 'would not only make possible a major improvement in our economic position but, at least as important, help to give dignity to many of our young people who today look upon themselves as failures. Getting the education right would improve the quality of life (not just livelihood) for the next generation and beyond.'

Whether or not one agrees with the particular analysis and solutions offered by the Commission (and there are alternatives), the issues raised by its members, Eric Bolton and many others are surely those that schools - meaning all those involved - should be addressing.

This chapter started with a reference to journeys, and has drawn attention to the agreement that exists about the destination (in terms of raising standards) for which our school system should be heading. There is plainly disagreement about the route, and even some about the starting point. There is obviously a lot to be discussed, therefore, if the destination is to be reached other than by chance.

Throughout, this book has sought to point out the possible disadvantages and dangers of opting out as the route to changing the school system; at the start of the previous chapter, we saw that opting out is certainly not established as the route that most schools (or even most secondary schools) are following - and that, even where they are, it is not with the support of a majority of parents. The starting point, then, cannot be that opting out is in any way inevitable. However, I have also acknowledged the reasons for which schools do look in that direction, and the inevitability that more will do so.

But ultimately, there seems little logic in choosing to opt out. It is hard to see what advantage it can bring to schools or the nation. At best, the increased independence and financial gain - relative to other schools operating either under LMS or with GM status if it spreads far - will be short-lived and transient; in any event, the gains will not be sufficient to significantly benefit anyone, even present pupils, beyond the very short-term. At worst, if it spreads significantly, it could - as its advocates intend - unleash a fundamental change in the underlying philosophy of our school system - and society - that would be more far-reaching than any change since the introduction of universal education provision; but a change that would be a massive step backwards.

The social consequences of the divisions that could all too easily occur would be such that there would be not gainers and losers, but only losers - for even those who, superficially, appeared to gain from being on the privileged side of the increasing divide would find their gains increasingly the target of the dispossessed. Defending them would occupy an increasing proportion of concern, energy and resources. Could it possibly be worth the effort? Is moving in that direction worth the risk? Is that really the sort of future any of us - from whichever side of the divide - really want our children to inherit? Do we really want to have to worry about which side of the divide they may end up on? The only way to avoid that anxiety is to ensure that we do not create the situation.

It has been a theme of the Government for some years, at least in its rhetoric, under both Mrs Thatcher and Mr Major, that its purpose is to empower the people. Through the publication of the White Paper and further legislation on schools, the Government (perhaps with some reluctance?) has given the people the opportunity to take control of the situation and to set their own agenda for change. It should, of course, be delighted if they choose to do so.

Over the course of the next year or so, we shall certainly see the future pattern of school provision in England and Wales largely determined by the public debate that takes place during that time. (What happens in Scotland may well follow a similar pattern.) We shall also see the extent to which 'the people' express a view during that debate - and the extent to which the government listens.

In the absence of any properly organised or recognised national representative body for parents - the crucial group of 'the people' so far as education is concerned - the Government has tended to dismiss opposition to its policies as coming from, or inspired by, 'self-interest groups' of professionals or 'politically motivated' and 'unrepresentative' minorities. The procedures for opting out, however, offer an almost unique opportunity to counter such suggestions. They centre around a ballot of parents, who are thus able to express - individually - their views in a way that must be recognised as representative.

If the initiative is taken successfully to turn the discussion away from that of opting out in individual schools towards that of how the school system as a whole can be improved in ways over which a broad consensus actually exists (or once again can be constructed) then the number of ballots is likely to remain fairly small. That in itself will oblige the policy makers to address these other, more pressing priorities. If the ballots that are held, or at least an increasing proportion of them, reject opting out as the right way forward, then the case will be strengthened greatly - and the chance of achieving real progress on a consensual basis will be considerably enhanced.

The crucial factors that will determine the direction in which the situation develops are the extent to which the issue can be made one of national importance; and to which parents, in particular, become aware of the significance and urgency of the matter; it will also depend on whether the issue can be broadened beyond the short-term self-interest of individual schools - and whether, on a sufficiently large scale, people who have not been accustomed to taking part in great numbers in the discussion of how schools are run can be persuaded, and given the confidence, to do so. Knowledge and information are a great boost to confidence; those who have them *must* share them with those who do not. Although many people involved in schools are fatigued by change, or maybe by campaigning against particular changes, it is essential that no effort is now spared in making the most of this decisive, and somewhat unexpected, opportunity to influence the direction of the further change that is inevitable.

The future of schools depends upon the choice that is made over opting out.

NOTES

1   Preface, *Every Child in Britain*, Report of the Channel 4 Commission, 1991.
2   The Commission did not deal with private education, but did feel that much of its report was equally applicable to Scotland, where the education system is somewhat different.
3   An abridged version of Mr Bolton's speech appeared in *Education* and the *TES*, July 1992.

INDEX